TABLE OF

TABLE OF CONTENTS

How To Take A Breath

Reduce Stress And Improve Performance By Breathing Well

Tania Clifton-Smith
Trailblazing NZ Clinician & Educator In
Breathing For Health & Wellness

16pt

Read How You Want
LARGE PRINT BOOKS, BRAILLE & DAISY

Copyright Page from the Original Book

Disclaimer

The author has made considerable effort to ensure the information contained in this book is accurate. The information provided is designed to increase awareness and initiate self-care but not to replace your health care provider. Please see a medical health care practitioner if you require more assistance.

This book is dedicated to my many patients with thanks.

'When in doubt, breathe out.'

INTRODUCTION

THE NEED TO BREATHE

Over the last three decades my work in the field of breathing pattern disorders, breathing dysfunction and hyperventilation has been rich. My background training in physical education and physiotherapy has provided an ideal foundation for this field of practice and I have never stopped learning. My journey in this field began treating the literati, glitterati and high achievers at the top of their professions in London in the late 1980s. These clients had all been diagnosed with exhaustion, burnout and chronic hyperventilation syndrome (CHVS). Another wing of the practice was the treatment of survivors of torture. This group was also suffering from exhaustion and CHVS, but with added severe psychological trauma and pain. My learning curve was steep, challenging and stimulating, and I was hooked.

Working with both groups, as well as developing some unique therapeutic skills, I also gained priceless experience that covered the spectrum of what it is to be human. I also learnt that my background in physiotherapy and physical education was not enough for me to be able to understand and treat such conditions. There began my never-ending thirst for knowledge, honing of skills and people-contact in this field. One kind friend has even labelled me a self-confessed course-a-holic in the field of breathing!

Since then, my clinical practice has explored many aspects of breathing dysfunction. From the purely mechanical—for example, mouth breathing in children, and back and neck pain driven by breathing pattern dysfunction—to elite athletes who have postural breathing problems on a quest to move faster, to individuals with biochemical imbalances making them sensitive to all stressors as a result of having lower blood carbon dioxide levels than normal. Many fall into this common, silent, unknown category. I've also sought to understand the body's neuropsycho-physiology, which affects thoughts and emotions and includes areas such as insomnia, panic attacks and overwhelming stress. One thing I know for sure is you cannot breathe well and be experiencing panic—it's physiologically impossible.

Most people don't know that breathing is also connected with movement, sleep, bowel motions, feelings, thoughts, general health and performance, and voice control. There is more to breathing than just breathing in and breathing out. Breathing is the first step to overall health, movement and well-being.

So, why this book and why now? Because I don't believe the message of the importance of breathing well is being heard. Breathing well has a profound effect on health and well-being and it is not as simple as some would like to imagine. Breathing is complex. There are many things that affect the way we breathe, and the way we breathe will affect many things.

Generalised breathing protocols do *not* fit everyone, especially if there is some dysfunction. Those people need an individualised, tailor-made programme. However, there are general principles that apply to many people—if they know what to look for. It is these simple principles I plan to outline in this book. The rest is best left to the medical experts in this field.

A word of caution: if you're trying the exercises suggested in this book and they're not working or you feel worse, please see a medical professional.

In today's society, pressure is paramount, change is inevitable, and the speed and volume of communication is only going to increase. Those with the tools, resilience and the ability to adapt will thrive. Those without, will not. It's as simple as that.

As a clinician, I am deeply passionate about the importance of breathing well and still see it as an untapped tool that everyone has immediate access to, which will help improve health and well-being. Breathing is the most fundamental function to help regulate many systems. It's a key to better self-understanding. We can tune into it anywhere and anytime, and it is drug-free.

In our clinic, we say: 'Breathing is the conductor of the orchestra'. It influences all the body's organs and functions. Extended time without air is deadly, and we need to keep breathing for survival. Ultimately, everything the body does is to ensure cells are well oxygenated, carbon dioxide balanced and we continue breathing.

Over the past decade, science and the medical profession have started taking note and now more physicians will consider breathing therapies/breathing rehabilitation as treatment options for numerous conditions and disorders.

Because there are many things that drive altered breathing, some of which are driven by a disease base and some that are not, it helps to unpack the puzzle of why an individual's breathing changes, as this then often determines the treatment programme. Clinically, I've seen the age of clients get younger and younger—in particular, those experiencing stress, anxiety and panic-related issues. This concerns and frustrates me. Breathing awareness and simple strategies should be taught immediately to everyone presenting with symptoms. They can be taught instead of or in conjunction with cognitive thought strategies and medication.

We've had the mindfulness wave. This is a start. Breathing therapies are similar but distinctly different, and for many they are an as yet untapped resource.

Breathing well affects all our body's systems. All areas of the body are interconnected, and if we are breathing well, we'll experience many positive improvements, which will be highlighted over the course of this book. These include:

- enhanced posture, stability and vocal quality
- better digestion, and gut and bowel movements
- improved cardiovascular and lymphatic flows
- improved sleep
- better regulation of the nervous system

- improved focus, attention and clarity of thought
- enhanced cellular action and metabolism
- an ability to relax and calm an anxious mind
- a boosting of the immune system
- better regulation of breathlessness and processing of pain
- greater self-regulation, which is the skill of learning how to soothe and calm ourselves—a process usually learnt from an early age.

A conference of all the human faculties met and first had to decide who would be in charge.

First, sight shined through and put in its bid, with captivating, vivid images that left all enraptured.

Smell then released fragrant scents through the air that made everyone tingle with anticipation.

But taste exceeded this with luscious flavours from around the globe.

Not to be deafened, hearing created wonderful harmonies that brought everyone to tears while the body's senses yielded incredible sensations that had all in ecstasy.

Then the mind turned on, spinning out deep and beautiful intellectual theories and truths.

Finally, along came the breath—not even one of the senses—and said it wanted to be in charge. All it had to show was its simple in and out breath—not impressive enough to all the others.

So, all the faculties ignored the breath and got into a tremendous argument about which of the others would be chosen.

The breath, disappointed, decided to leave.

And as it did, the images began to fade, the tastes lost their savour, sounds diminished, the mind became feeble.

'Wait!' the senses called out. 'Come back, and you can lead.'

And the breath returned and took its proper place...

—from the Brihadaranyaka Upanishad, 9–6BCE

CHAPTER 1

WHAT'S ALL THE FUSS ABOUT?

'I breathe in and I breathe out, I've done it my whole life—how can something that simple be the problem?'

Breathing is so much more than respiration

The respiratory system involves the airways and the exchange of gases between the air and the blood, and between the blood and the body's cells. The main function of respiration is to provide cells with oxygen and to remove the correct amount of carbon dioxide. But breathing is so much more than this. It affects the whole body, from the rhythm of brain function to body stability, to co-ordination and vocalisation, to our moods, emotions and even the way we think.

How to get breath to work well for you is one of the human body's best-kept secrets—until now!

After years of working in this field, I take it for granted that everyone knows how important breathing is and how fundamental it is for health, so I am still amazed when clients return for their first follow-up session and say things like:

> 'My thoughts have slowed. I can focus for longer and I haven't been as reactive and hyper as I usually am.'

> 'I'm less anxious.'

> 'My body feels settled.'

> 'My sleep is much deeper.'

> 'I'm not as breathless.'

> 'I can run further and faster.'

> 'Wow! I didn't know breathing could make that much of a difference!'

This chapter will explain how each of those improvements can happen when we breathe better.

How does breathing affect our thoughts, focus and reactions?

Our autonomic nervous system governs the automatic functions of our bodies, such as our heart rate, blood pressure, digestion and the blood flow to our muscles and brain. The role of this system is to keep us in balance, which is known as a state of homeostasis. In short, it ensures we're ready for all situations.

The autonomic nervous system regulates certain body processes. It is made up of two opposing networks—the parasympathetic branch and the sympathetic branch—and a third branch called the enteric system, which has a direct link to the gut. The enteric system is largely regulated by the two main branches. It is also influenced by neurotransmitters, which transmit signals across cells to stop and start messages.

For example, a couple of the key gut neurotransmitters are serotonin and dopamine. Serotonin stabilises our mood and feelings of happiness, and dopamine is associated with our reward centre. Both are very important neurotransmitters in how we feel and what drives our behaviour. Dopamine and serotonin are both produced in the gut as well as the brain. Breathing well has been proven to enrich the blood flow to the gut, thereby stabilising and assisting in the healthy production of these neurotransmitters.

Breathing well at rest is breathing in and out of the nose while your belly moves with a slow rate—'nose, low (belly) and slow'. This healthy way of breathing will activate and calm the part of the autonomic nervous system called the parasympathetic branch.

The parasympathetic branch is the relaxing branch of the autonomic nervous system, while the sympathetic branch is the stimulating one. Clinically, we refer to the parasympathetic branch as being in the green zone. In this zone, breathing is calm, rhythmical and regular and our body reflects this.

If this resting breathing pattern is disrupted, such as when breathing faster, with a bigger volume, or using held and/or dysregulated breaths, the sympathetic branch will dominate. We refer to this as being in the red zone. In this zone, adrenaline infiltrates our body and we are pumped, primed and ready for action.

When we're calm, our gut has a full blood supply as do our reproductive organs and brain. This state is associated with the healthy digestion of food, and increased libido, enabling reproduction, hence the term, 'rest, and digest and reproduce'.

When calm, a hormone called acetylcholine is released to slow the heart rate, and our blood pressure is regulated. Our body and brain then have a good blood supply, allowing full oxygenation to all cells. It is believed that it is from this state that our best and brightest ideas originate as the brain is well oxygenated. In essence, it promotes resting, nourishing and the repair aspects for our body.

When we sense a threat, either real or perceived, our body sends a message to the brain to get ready to fight, flee or even freeze. When this happens, blood is diverted away from the gut and brain, and we certainly don't need to reproduce in the height of battle, so the relaxed systems switch off and the alert system switches on ready for action moving into the red zone, which is the sympathetic branch.

Breathing can regulate and trigger both of these branches—the parasympathetic and sympathetic branches of the nervous system. The breath acts as a switch with the ability to transition between the green and red zones.

In the green zone, you're breathing calmly at rest. Your breathing is effortless, through the nose, slow, and the rate is low (six to twelve breaths per minute for an adult) and regular. If your breathing is like this, you are unlikely to be stressed.

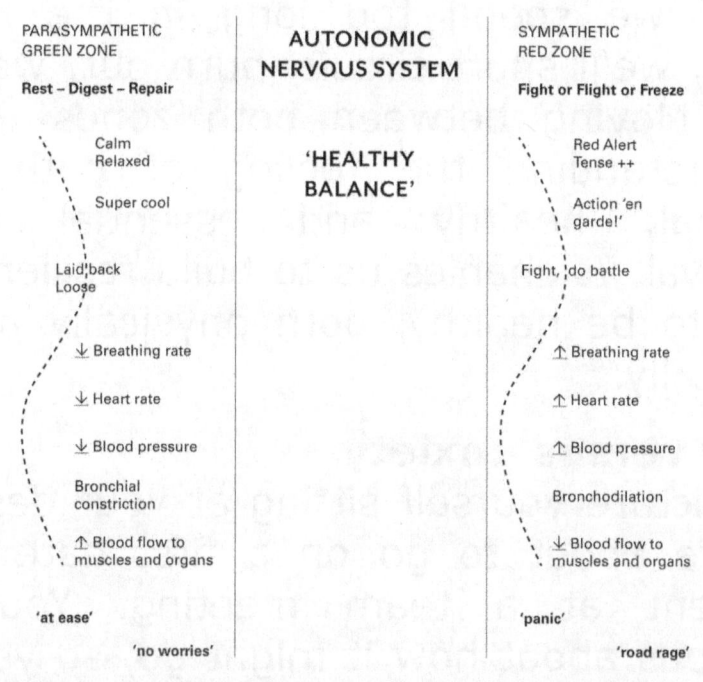

PARASYMPATHETIC GREEN ZONE	AUTONOMIC NERVOUS SYSTEM	SYMPATHETIC RED ZONE
Rest – Digest – Repair		**Fight or Flight or Freeze**
Calm Relaxed	'HEALTHY BALANCE'	Red Alert Tense ++
Super cool		Action 'en garde!'
Laid back Loose		Fight, do battle
↓ Breathing rate		↑ Breathing rate
↓ Heart rate		↑ Heart rate
↓ Blood pressure		↑ Blood pressure
Bronchial constriction		Bronchodilation
↑ Blood flow to muscles and organs		↓ Blood flow to muscles and organs
'at ease'		'panic'
'no worries'		'road rage'

Green zone: Breathing is rhythmical, regular, through the nose and into the belly. Red zone: Breathing is rapid, irregular, often into the upper chest and maybe through the mouth.

However, if your breathing changes to become faster, more irregular and with bigger volumes, especially if you're resting, it's likely you've been shot up with adrenaline and you're ready to react to any potential threat. This means you've moved into the red zone. Other signs of heading to the red zone are chaotic patterns and prolonged breath-holding.

If we spend too long in the red zone, we'll short-circuit, burn out, wear out. Moving between both zones and understanding the feeling of both is normal, healthy and essential for survival. It enables us to build resilience and to be healthy, both physically and mentally.

Fear versus anxiety

Picture yourself sitting at your desk. You're about to go on a first date or present at a team meeting. You're nervous about how it might go, so your brain is conjuring up a whole lot of possible scenarios—some good and some not so good. You start to sweat a little bit and start to worry about saying the wrong thing or spilling food down yourself. The more you think about what could go wrong, the more anxious you become, which threatens to spoil the date or the meeting before you even get there.

The problem is our brain and body have not yet worked out the difference between perceived and real threats. Perceived threats can create a state of anxiety, which is different from the true fear that this system was designed to deal with.

True fear will set in when we are in real and immediate danger. For example, if your car's brakes fail while you're driving, or you're being held at gunpoint or chased by a wild animal, that's when true fear kicks in.

Meanwhile, anxiety is a normal experience, but when it is prolonged or goes into overdrive, it can create havoc. It does this by creating sensations of true fear in potentially fear-generating scenarios. For example, some people develop a fear of flying because of the potential of what might go wrong, and some people just worry for the sake of worrying.

The most common fears are social phobias in which excessive worry can create fear of otherwise normal situations, like being asked to speak in public. Often, it is the worry of the symptoms rather than the event that can create this self-perpetuating cycle of anxiety and fear.

A report from the World Health Organization (WHO) released in 2017 estimated 284 million people experienced an anxiety disorder, making it the most prevalent mental health or neuro-developmental disorder globally. As a result of the global spread of COVID-19, this figure skyrocketed in 2020.

In June 2020, the US's Department of Health and Human Services' Centers for Disease Control and Prevention (CDC) reported that 40 per cent of adults in the United States reported experiencing issues with mental health and substance abuse. These statistics are mirrored in many other countries. Anxiety disorders are highly treatable, and awareness of breathing is an aspect that should be included in treatment and prevention.

Rachel, a 35-year-old legal executive, presented with palpitations, poor sleep and general anxiety. She had no idea how tight and tense she was or that she was continuously holding her breath, especially at work. She also wore extremely tight clothes and constantly clenched her belly in an effort to look thinner. It took her six weeks before she was able to recognise when she was tensing her body and holding her breath. Now her energy has improved, she has better clarity of thought and she's not as tense as she once was.

It's important to know that anxiety is not just a mind phenomenon. It's a bodily reaction that prepares us for action. Increased breathing will prepare the body to react to danger or perceived threat.

TRY THIS

Stop
Feel your breath in this instant.
Are you holding your breath?
If so, is it on the in or the out breath?

If you were holding your breath, in particular on the in breath, your body was sending a message to your brain to get ready for action and moving you towards the red zone. Your neck, shoulder and chest muscles were working with no good reason. Your gut started to clench, and your mind was searching for the reason for the high-alert signal.

If you were holding your breath on the out breath, these signals were still there but not as strongly.

Awareness of this unconscious daily habit is essential to break this cycle and teach your body the difference between true fear and perceived fear (anxiety). This takes time as, in the Western world, we're not great at listening to our bodies.

So now, just pause.

Breathe out.

Try to relax your gut (belly), your shoulders and your legs. Give them a wiggle, move them.

Slowly breathe in through your nose, and try to allow your belly to rise when you breathe in.

Then let the breath fall out.

Smile and continue reading.

This exercise involves literally having a breather. It is only the beginning of awareness into feeling how you breathe, so don't worry if this felt foreign or confusing, as hopefully by the end of the book this will be starting to come more naturally.

Over-breathing and breathing dysfunction drop the level of carbon dioxide in our blood. It's this drop that causes a chemical change in the body, thereby triggering a move into the red zone. The brain receives the signal to panic so that the body reacts in order to keep breathing and therefore stay alive.

How can breathing make your body feel calm and less tense?

Breathing well requires a healthy postural alignment, which is a bit like stacking blocks. If the blocks are lined up in an orderly manner, they will be stronger and more stable, thereby providing a good framework. In the case of the body, this involves providing an efficient framework so the breathing muscles can pump and move effectively, as can all the muscles surrounding them. This effective and efficient pumping system requires less energy while ensuring the muscles are well supplied with oxygen and that lactic acid (the by-product of movement) is removed effectively. This keeps muscles tension-free and helps the body to remain calm.

Think of the chest and the torso (abdomen) as if they're two squares stacked one on top of the other. Inside each of the squares is a cavity.

The top one is the intrathoracic cavity, which houses the lungs and heart. The lungs span from the top of your collarbone to the bottom of your ribcage when fully inflated.

The vocal folds (which used to be known as the vocal cords) sit at the top of the intrathoracic cavity and act like a pressure valve, thereby creating the voice, regulating airflow and protecting the airways from choking.

The bottom square is the intra-abdominal cavity, which houses the gut, intestines, spleen, liver, kidneys, bladder and reproductive organs. At the bottom of this cavity sit the pelvic floor muscles, which create the lower support system for the pelvic organs while also helping to control the bladder, the bowel and sexual organs. Speech, voice and all things pelvic-floor-related are connected and rely on the integrity of the system to function optimally.

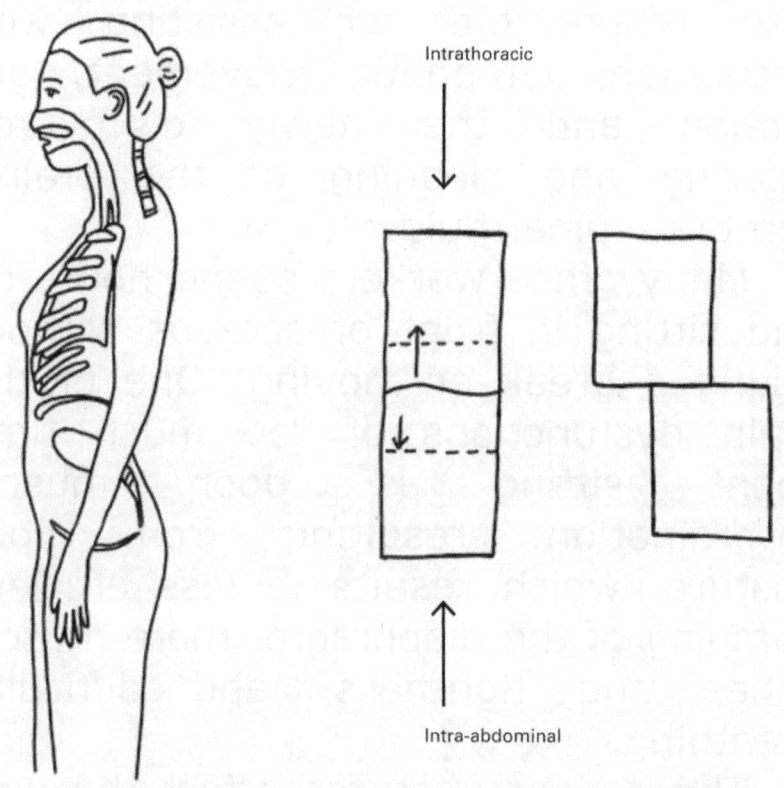

Intrathoracic

Intra-abdominal

The diaphragm (the main breathing muscle) sits in the middle of the two squares, and it has the ability to move up and down, changing the pressure within each space.

With each breath, the muscles co-ordinate to enable movement, but also create pressure changes within the various cavities. The diaphragm acts as a pump in the middle. The pumping action allows pressure changes to bring air in and out of the lungs, plus it's also responsible for assisting with circulation, lymphatic movement, gut motion and the newly discovered clearing and cleaning of the brain's cerebral spinal fluid.

Many office workers spend hours on end sitting in front of screens without taking a break or moving. One of the main dysfunctions of too much time spent sitting is poor muscle co-ordination, resulting from poor posture, which results in less efficient pumping of the diaphragm, more muscle aches and tightness, and difficulty breathing.

These poor postures affect the way we breathe, and, in return, this moves us towards the red zone as muscle nerve messages become overactive, sending muscles the signal to tense up and get ready for action—a double whammy, which can cause tight, tense, sore muscles, among other problems.

As physiotherapists, we encourage everyone to move and move often. Research suggests that people should get up and move every 30 minutes. Sitting for lengthy periods is now considered to increase the risk of chronic health problems.

Sixteen-year-old Annabel started experiencing neck and shoulder pain, which was not fixed by conventional manual therapies. When attention was paid to the way she breathed, and her posture when using electronics, and to strengthening her diaphragm muscle, her neck and shoulder discomfort ceased.

How does breathing affect sleep?

The way we breathe has a major impact on our sleep. Research has shown that breathing well is essential for healthy sleep. The nasal breathing cycle is synchronised to our brain waves during sleep, so nasal health is paramount. When we sleep, we alternate between breathing through the right and the left nostrils. This alternating rhythm, which is a natural rhythm also seen throughout the day, is essential for good sleep and correlates to different phases of the sleep cycle.

How we breathe during the day will affect how we breathe at night, especially if we spend our days in the red zone. If we've been on red alert all day, we won't revert to the green zone just because we're asleep. Switching back to the green zone requires awareness and tuning into our breath.

When we sleep, we go through a four-stage, 90-minute cycle known as our ultradian sleep rhythm. This consists of rapid eye movement (REM) and non-rapid eye movement (NREM) sleep. The REM phase is controlled by the limbic system, which is the system that deals with emotions and memory. The unconscious REM phase is when our brain makes sense of what's been happening in our daily life and organises experiences somewhat like a filing system. During the REM phase, all skeletal muscles apart from the diaphragm are paralysed.

If your neck and shoulder muscles do a lot of the work of breathing during the day, this does not change when we sleep, so during REM sleep, when these muscles become paralysed, your body does not cope well as it struggles to make sense of how to breathe as it has been using the wrong muscles for breathing. If this is the case, when the neck and shoulder muscles become paralysed, this will often cause you to wake, have a restless sleep or even snore.

It's even worse for those with a condition called sleep apnoea. In these cases, this confusion will trigger the body back to a different stage of sleep to ensure breathing continues. Fractured sleep can be catastrophic, as all the phases and stages of sleep are important for normal functioning, especially for the immune system. Breathing well is the key function to help restore poor sleep habits.

John, 56 years old, presented with poor sleep, snoring, fatigue and generally feeling 'rough and unrefreshed'. He was slightly overweight and had a stressful job that involved a lot of time spent on the phone. John was a very reversed breather. He breathed predominantly into his upper chest. He also admitted to holding in his belly as he had put on weight, plus he had a stuffy nose, which caused him to mouth breathe.

John began a routine of daily nasal rinsing, breathing re-education (chapter 8) and doing a calm-down, bliss-out exercise before sleep. Within three weeks, John started sleeping through the night and waking feeling more refreshed. His energy levels improved and, thankfully for his wife, his snoring stopped.

'I am not as breathless'

It's really scary when you can't breathe. The way we breathe, the pattern of our breathing, is significant in triggering breathlessness.

There are many reasons why breathlessness occurs. It is an individually experienced sensation. Breathlessness may be caused by something that needs medical treatment, like cardiac or lung disease. It can also be a sensation experienced depending on how you are breathing. For example, if you hold your breath when running upstairs, you may feel breathless, or if you mouth or chest breathe this can cause a sensation of breathlessness.

Other factors associated with breathlessness are respiratory disorders, panic, anxiety, movement and breathing dysregulation.

Unco-ordinated running and breathing cadence will cause breathlessness, as will reaching the end of one's aerobic threshold. Cadence is the rhythm in which we move. When movement and breathing are synchronised, our bodily systems will work in harmony (see chapter 9).

When we reach our anaerobic threshold during exercise, lactate, which is a by-product of exercise, reaches a maximum level, causing the body to reduce its chemical efficiency by sending less oxygen to the tissues.

Breathing well will help reduce the sensation of breathlessness, as you will learn throughout this book.

CAUSES OF BREATHLESSNESS (DYSPNOEA)

PHYSIOLOGY: Your lungs and airways have a disease or are irritated. For example, you might have too much phlegm, tight inflamed airways with asthma, or be mouth breathing because you have a blocked nose.

PSYCHOPHYSIOLOGY: You might be anxious, fearful, overwhelmed, excited or worried, or you might have a busy brain.

MECHANICAL: You may be holding your breath when you move, so movement and breathing are not co-ordinated. You may also be over-breathing into the upper chest, which allows little room for more air.

EXERCISE: You may be unfit when exercising. Or have reached your anaerobic threshold.

Ian is 75 years old and has chronic lung disease. He came to see me as a result of his breathlessness when walking up inclines. His main problem was that he'd never learnt the fundamentals of lung health for his disease, including chest clearance and breathing well at rest and during movement. He wasn't clearing his lungs to make sure the mucus was removed. He was also holding his breath when walking and he had an irregular breathing pattern when at rest.

After a few sessions on chest clearance, breathing well at rest (chapter 8), rest positions for breathlessness and co-ordinated breathing when moving, Ian was able to manage the scary sensation of breathlessness. In fact, he tuned into it and learnt what his body was telling him. When he became breathless, he would pause, catch his breath and then move again. The main factor for him was to ensure he was co-ordinating his breath and movement, especially when going up stairs or inclines. He *also learnt to pace his steps and not to hold his breath.*

'I can run further and faster'

Breathlessness during exercise is a normal sensation. However, if the pattern of breathing and the co-ordination of movement is not synchronised, this can increase the sensation of breathlessness and limit exercise tolerance prematurely. Erratic breathing patterns gobble up more oxygen, which further limits exercise. It's no wonder that with efficient patterns and timed cadence, you can run further and faster. The strengthening of the diaphragm also makes a major difference in these cases.

Zac is 25 and he's a triathlete. He came to see me because he wanted to improve his swim time. It soon became clear that Zac wasn't great at relaxing, as he thought downtime was the same as relaxation. On examination using real-time ultrasound, he was also found to have a thinner diaphragm than he should have. This indicated that he wasn't breathing with the efficient pattern usually seen in an elite athlete. Treatment covered basic breathing retraining (chapter 8), developing relaxation skills, inspiratory muscle training to strengthen his diaphragm, and reinforcing an efficient motor pattern. Within three weeks, he noticed changes, and within six weeks, he was achieving personal-best times in the pool.

'Wow! I didn't know breathing could make that much of a difference'

Breathing well involves using the optimal breathing pattern for any given situation. Breathing patterns adapt to the appropriate demands from the body for the given activity or situation, and will help regulate the physiology of the body while also influencing the mind. When breathing is disrupted and becomes dysfunctional, significant issues can arise. The fixes are not always quick. They take time, repetition and dedication, but they are always worth the effort.

CHAPTER 2

WHY BREATHE WELL?

As the field of work around breathing has expanded, so has the number of people giving us advice on how to breathe and how not to breathe, what good breathing is and what bad breathing is. 'Good' or 'bad' is not the key—it's all about breathing well for your situation, age and stage of life. Whether you're an elite athlete, a toddler having a tantrum, a person having a panic attack, a long-haul post-viral fatigue sufferer or a terminal cancer patient, you can still breathe well to suit what's happening in your life. Most importantly, breathing well is all about you. It is an individual experience as there is no quick fix that works for everyone.

Breathing can develop and it can adapt either to enhance and build resilience or to make you sick, leaving you feeling more tired and anxious.

THE SECONDARY
(ACCESSORY)
BREATHING MUSCLES
30% body energy use

THE PRIMARY
BREATHING MUSCLES
5% body energy use

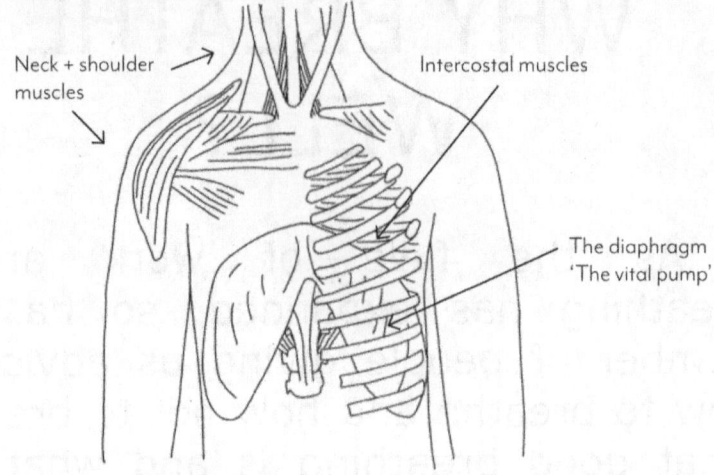

Neck + shoulder
muscles

Intercostal muscles

The diaphragm
'The vital pump'

The mechanical advantages of breathing well

The structure and mechanics of the body are designed so that, at rest, we breathe in and out using our nose in conjunction with the power of a muscle called the diaphragm, which is often called 'the vital pump'. Nasal breathing with a healthy postural alignment enhances optimal diaphragm movement with effortless muscle work. This is the basis of breathing well at rest and is known as abdominal breathing.

However, many people call it diaphragm breathing or belly breathing.

The diaphragm draws air into the lungs as easily as a syringe draws up fluid. It is the main primary breathing muscle and is responsible for 80–90 per cent of the work done during quiet breathing. The remaining 10–20 per cent is carried out by the muscles attached to your ribcage.

The breathing muscles are grouped into the primary and accessory muscles. The primary muscles are those used all the time, including the diaphragm and the intercostal muscles. These are the muscles between the ribs, which help the ribcage move. The secondary muscles, also known as the accessory or emergency muscles, are those of the neck, shoulders and trunk. The accessory muscles are only called upon in certain situations such as during exercise or when we are required to move larger amounts of air or assist with stability.

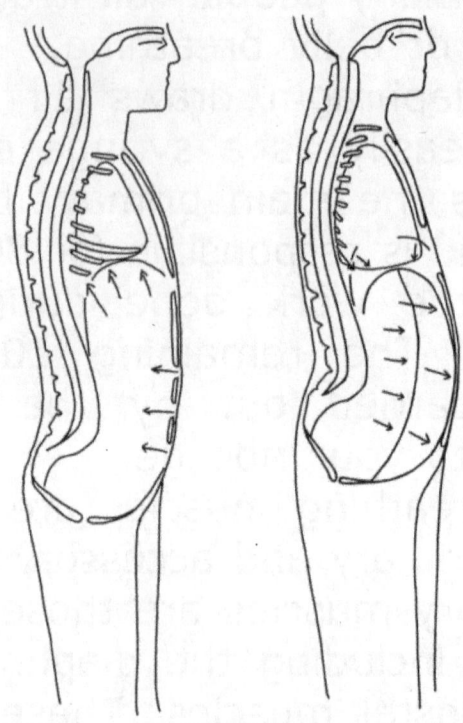

It takes less than five per cent of your body's energy to use your diaphragm muscle to breathe. When you breathe using the muscles in your shoulders and neck, it can use up to 30 per cent of your body's energy.

Breathing well mechanically saves energy and ensures oxygen goes to the necessary muscles and organs. It also draws the air to the lower lobes of the lungs, which are much more oxygen rich than the upper lobes. The efficient pumping action creates healthy pressure regulation between the top (intrathoracic) and bottom (intra-abdominal) cavities within the body (see section entitled "How can breathing make your body feel calm and less tense?"). The vocal folds form the top of the intrathoracic cavity and the diaphragm is at the bottom of it. Therefore, pressure changes within this cavity will have an effect on our voice. The heart also sits in this cavity and is attached to the diaphragm via a membranous sac, which encapsulates it. The heart sits to the left of the chest and moves with each healthy breath.

When we breathe in (inhale) and the diaphragm moves downwards, the heart contracts, and when we breathe out (exhale) and the diaphragm moves upwards, the heart relaxes. This pressure change affects the blood flow and the firing of receptors in the heart. These receptors are known as the baroreceptors and they determine blood pressure, so the way we breathe contributes to our heart health.

Not only does the diaphragm pump help regulate blood pressure and blood flow, it also plays a part in regulating heart rate variability, which is the variation in the intervals between consecutive heartbeats. Many people think their hearts beat absolutely regularly but there is usually a variation of milliseconds in the time between each beat. This difference is often referred to as the R-R interval. It is known to play a role in firing of various parts of the brain. Some specialists are adamant that this is the true determinant of heart health.

The concept is that, in a healthy heart, this rate varies—the bigger the variation, the better. Why is this important? We know the way we breathe affects the level of variation. A slower breath rate of around five to seven breaths per minute is thought to be the ideal breathing rate for the healthiest and most robust variation. This is known as resonance frequency breathing, or coherent breathing, and this is the ultimate passage to the green zone. When breathing like this, the nervous system, respiratory system and cardiovascular system are all working effectively together.

When you have a coherent breathing rhythm the heart rate R-R wave changes continuously, and this is considered the gold standard of calm and body homeostasis (internal balance). Do not go straight to trying to breathe at five to seven breaths per minute. This should be done as part of a step-by-step process and as an exercise when trying to achieve a calm state.

How does this happen?

The baroreceptors are the stretch receptors on the heart, and they respond to movement, in particular the movement of the diaphragm and pressure changes within the chest cavity. When breathing at a rate of five to seven abdominal breaths per minute, the pressure variation triggers the heart receptors to respond with a certain frequency and vibration. This sends a message back to the brain creating a neurochemical frequency of 0.1 Hz. It's this brain frequency and vibration that affect nerve activity and light up the brain centres, in particular, the prefrontal cortex.

The prefrontal cortex is responsible for planning complex behaviour, expression, decision-making and moderating social behaviour. In other words, how we breathe can affect the way we think, feel and behave. It also plays a major role in the blood supply to the brain, and we know the brain is fuelled by oxygen.

Breath affects the baroreflex, a reflex that helps to maintain blood pressure. Resonance occurs at approximately a 10-second breath cycle, which is approximately six breaths per minute.

The intra-abdominal cavity

The intra-abdominal cavity is the cavity below the diaphragm. The floor of this cavity is the pelvic floor, the front is the abdominal muscles, and the back is the deep back muscles. They all work together dominated by the movement of the diaphragm. The pressure change effect in this cavity when breathing will affect all of the structures contained in there, as well as systems sensitive to pressure such as the cardiovascular and lymphatic pumps.

It micro-massages the gut and intestinal contents. It brings fresh blood to organs and helps to remove toxins. It also has a major role in the return of blood from the veins of the lower limbs and the lymphatic fluid, which carries waste products, plus pumping the brain fluid known as cerebrospinal fluid (CSF).

CSF is the fluid that cushions and protects the brain. It feeds the brain with nutrients and removes the brain's waste products. It's been discovered only in the past decade that when we inhale, fluid flows into the brain, and when we exhale, fluid flows out of the brain. So, our breathing pattern is essential for cleaning out the brain.

Energy-efficient breathing patterns create the adequate internal pressure required for organ health. It's a bit like cleaning out a blocked drain. If a drain is blocked and we use a weak plunging action to unblock it, it won't work, but a strong plunging action will clear the drain and keep things flowing. It's the same for the pumping of the diaphragm during abdominal breathing. A strong diaphragm pump is healthy.

MECHANICAL ADVANTAGES OF BREATHING WELL

- Better posture
- Energy-efficient movement patterns
- Improved vocalisation/speech
- Improved heart tone
- A strong, healthy cardiovascular pump
- Better gut movement and health
- Lymphatic pump (toxin removal pump)
- Pumps cerebrospinal fluid (fluid supporting brain health)

The chemical advantages of breathing well

The importance of carbon dioxide

Although we all know how vital oxygen (O_2) is, many people don't understand the importance of the carbon dioxide (CO_2) in our bodies. It is the main regulator of our breathing, our nerve connections and the autonomic nervous system. It controls the blood flow to the brain, the size of the coronary artery vessels and the ability of blood to release or hold onto oxygen. It affects the removal of lactic acid, which is the waste product from the energy cycle, and it also has an effect on the release of histamine, which is involved in the inflammatory response.

The regulation of breathing is complex, but the body will do whatever it can to ensure you keep breathing. When we are in deep strife, higher centres in the brain take over the control of breathing; when CO_2 is too high, it triggers us to breathe, and when CO_2 is too low, we will faint to override conscious control.

The key physiological functions of breathing are to breathe in oxygen (O_2) and to breathe out the right amount of CO_2. These two functions ensure we maintain a stable body pH. The pH is the acid–alkaline balance in the blood and body. This preserves homeostasis, which is body balance, in particular at a cellular level.

For example, if we start to breathe in more oxygen than the body needs, by taking big breaths or breathing too fast at rest, the body will start to flush out carbon dioxide in the blood stream to make the pH stable and to maintain stability.

Ideal body chemistry

$O_2 \rightleftharpoons pH \rightleftharpoons CO_2$

When we breathe in too much O_2—for example, over-breathing at rest to keep the pH stable—the body will flush CO_2 out of the blood.

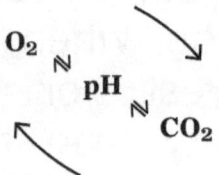

Often, when we are really unwell, this O_2–CO_2 balance is in constant flux so is constantly changing. For example, when we have a high temperature, we need to breathe faster to keep the body pH stable. This will result in an altered breathing pattern, which is an indicator that something is not right. A qualified therapist or health practitioner will be able to use clinical reasoning skills to assess whether this altered pattern is as a result of something serious happening or whether it is just a bad habit.

If symptoms persist and are not changed by the basic breathing routine (see chapter 8), please seek medical professional help.

Many of us over-breathe at rest for no medical reason. Over-breathing at rest means the way we are breathing does not match the activity we're doing. For example, breathing too fast, breathing into our upper chest, and/or mouth breathing when we are sitting still, so at rest, or during normal low-level activity, can flush too much carbon dioxide from the body.

FUNCTIONS OF CARBON DIOXIDE

- Regulates rate and depth of breathing.
- Controls blood flow to the brain.
- Affects haemoglobin uptake of oxygen. Haemoglobin is the protein in blood that carries oxygen.
- Affects coronary artery constriction.
- Governs nervous tissue activity.
- Regulates activity of the autonomic nervous system.
- Controls firing speed of nerves.
- Regulates and removes the byproduct of energy called lactate.
- Can affect mast cells and the related histamine release.

Low blood levels of CO2

If we maintain altered breathing patterns that have driven the O_2 too high, the body will try to compensate by flushing CO_2 out of the blood stream. If the altered pattern is sustained for some time, this will cause the blood level of CO_2 to drop lower than it should. When this happens, we will start to experience symptoms such as pins and needles, numbness in the lips, a racing heart and brain fog. These symptoms are the body's way of telling us to stop and take notice of what we are doing. Are we breathing right for the situation? Why are we over-breathing?

However, many of us are not great at listening to our bodies, so instead we'll panic when such symptoms start to occur as they can seem scary. This often creates a vicious cycle that can become established as a habitual pattern (see opposite). Dysfunctional breathing can become habitual and, with time, a carbon dioxide intolerance can occur.

Over-breathing pushes CO_2 levels to lower than normal, which tends to make the body tissues more alkaline. Tingling and light-headedness may be the first signs of this. Continued or chronic over-breathing becomes more complex as the body tries to adjust to this situation in the long term. The kidneys are called in to excrete bicarbonate (alkaline), to help retain normal body acidity. The drive to breathe faster becomes habitual as the body takes great pains to preserve a normal pH level. Carbon dioxide levels remain lowered and the respiratory centre in the brain learns to accept this. The rest of the body is not quite so accepting. It suffers. This is the vicious cycle of habitual breathing dysfunction.

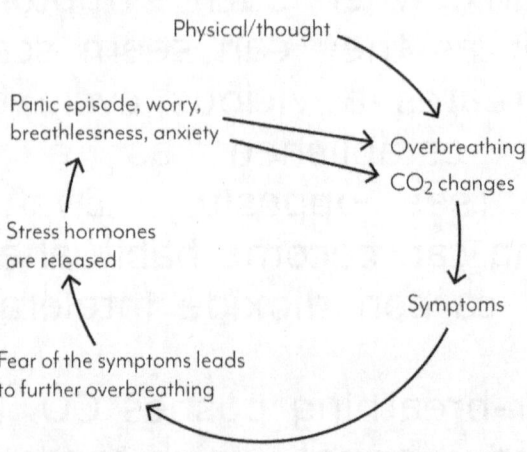

TRIGGER

Physical/thought

Panic episode, worry, breathlessness, anxiety

Overbreathing
CO_2 changes

Stress hormones are released

Symptoms

Fear of the symptoms leads to further overbreathing

BREAK THE VICIOUS CYCLE

SYMPTOMS OF OVER-BREATHING OR HYPERVENTILATION

- Feelings of 'air hunger', or not getting enough air
- Inability to take a deep breath
- Shortness of breath*
- Breathlessness*
- Cold hands and feet/tingling fingers
- Numbness in the hands, feet or mouth
- Frequent sighing/yawning
- Aching muscles and joints, especially in the neck and shoulders
- Upset or bloated stomach, nausea
- Blurred vision*
- Dizzy spells*
- Fatigue/exhaustion
- Disturbed or light sleep
- Tightness in the chest
- Chest pains*
- Erratic heartbeat*
- Panic attacks
- In extreme cases, cramps, tetany in the hands (hands clawing) and seizures

* See your doctor if you experience any of these symptoms.

Note: Many things feed into this chemical tipping point where we start to feel symptoms. If prolonged, the body can readjust to this new low limit, which is known as the new set point. To reset back to normal usually requires guidance from a therapist in breathing retraining.

Low blood levels of CO_2 will not harm us in the short term as the body will send signals that this is happening in the form of the symptoms listed above. Hopefully, we'll respond by listening to our body and altering our breathing pattern or paying attention to what our body needs.

Unfortunately, we often misinterpret these signals as something more sinister as our mind goes searching for a potential reason for the feelings. The mind calls upon the limbic system (the memory library) and looks for a reason as to why these symptoms are present. It searches for past fear situations; for example, running away from a barking dog or being told off as a child. The mind often then attaches to such memories, which is how phobias are established.

Sadly, we can get things so wrong sometimes, which means instead of listening to our body telling us why something is happening, we attach meaning to a situation that may not have anything to do with the initial symptoms.

The first key to any breathing dysfunction is to recognise this cycle and its triggers. Once we understand why it is happening we are then able to break it.

Results of prolonged low CO2

• **Reduction of blood flow to the brain**

Low CO_2 levels can cause symptoms and chemical dysregulation in the brain. When carbon dioxide levels drop even a tiny amount, there is a twofold reduction in blood flow to the brain. It's no wonder foggy brain, reduced processing and loss of clarity of thought can occur.

• Oxygen is not easily released to cells

When carbon dioxide is low, oxygen is bound tightly to the red blood cells because the body wants to hang on to the oxygen just in case the vital organs need it. This affects cell health and leads to further muscle fatigue.

• Blood vessels constrict

Blood vessels in the extremities (legs, feet, hands, lips) are reduced in size to help bring the blood back to the vital organs, such as the heart and lungs. This reduces blood flow to the extremities, and often causes tingling in those areas or leads to the hands and feet becoming cold and often clammy.

• The nervous system moves us towards the sympathetic or red zone

Over-breathing and low CO_2 suppress the parasympathetic (green zone) more than the sympathetic (red zone) so the red zone dominates.

• Lactate in muscles is not cleared as efficiently

Over-breathing drops the CO_2, so the body prepares for a possible surge of acid in the blood. The source of this acid is the lactate left by the expected exertion required as part of the body's fight or flight response to danger. Often, that danger is not real, and we remain inert resulting in a mismatch—our breathing becomes incompatible with the action we are doing. We're breathing like we're running but we're not.

The body prepares us by releasing acid into the blood, creating more lactate in the muscles. As a result, the muscles ache, particularly in the overused upper chest. These muscles are greedy for oxygen, stealing it away from lower back and leg muscles, which may cause more premature muscle fatigue.

Note: In post-viral fatigue and chronic fatigue syndromes, this is one of the mechanisms driving poor exercise tolerance and muscle lactate build-up.

• The nerve–muscle junction is stimulated, again preparing the body to run

This causes muscles to become tight and tense even when we are at rest.

• Mast cells release more histamine

High levels of histamine increase the body's sensitivity to allergy triggers, resulting in more sneezing, wheezing, welts and itching. The more histamine there is, the more we become inflamed. When mast cells are overactive they produce more histamine. Over-breathing destabilises mast cells.

In chronic cases of breathing dysfunction, the following can also occur:

- An inability to move lactic acid out of the muscles, as seen in chronic fatigue syndrome and long Covid post-exertional malaise (PEM).
- Altered electrolyte balance (calcium, potassium, magnesium) increases the likelihood of spasm and fatigue, and seizures have even been noted.

High CO2

Having a high level of carbon dioxide in the blood is known as hypercapnia. We'll also receive signals if the CO_2 is retained at levels that are too high beyond the normal limits. The main cause for high CO_2 levels is not breathing enough. This usually occurs with lung disease and electrolyte imbalance. CO_2 levels can also be higher if someone has trained themselves to breath-hold for an extended time; for example, free divers.

Reasons you might not be breathing enough

Under-breathing can cause high blood CO_2, and this can be caused by any of a number of factors.

Drugs

Analgesics and barbiturates have a sedating effect on our system, causing a decrease in the drive to breathe. These drugs are often given for anxiety or to those who suffer from pain problems in order to help restore breathing back to normal from a state of over-breathing. Hyperventilation leads to low levels of CO_2 in the blood, which can then cause an over-correction. The practice of breath-holding can be a useful way of raising the carbon dioxide levels back to normal. (See section entitled "Breath-hold breathing".)

Decreased oxygen to the brain (hypoxia)

This will decrease the respiratory drive, increasing blood levels of CO_2. If these levels are high enough, acute respiratory failure may occur, which is potentially life-threatening.

Damage to the nerves supplying the muscles of breathing

Trauma to the spinal cord or nerves, in diseases such as motor neurone disease where the muscles stop working over time.

Lung diseases

Patients with late-stage chronic obstructive pulmonary disease (COPD) are prone to CO_2 retention, meaning there are high levels of CO_2 in the blood stream. This triggers under-breathing.

Due to a poor ventilation–perfusion mismatch, more CO_2 is being built up in the blood stream than what should be excreted.

The psychological advantages of breathing well

The triune brain theory suggests that as we evolved we developed skills for higher levels of learning and functioning as well as communication and living in communities. The theory outlines three developmental stages.

The first is the primitive reptilian brain, which is all about survival—fight, flee or freeze, meaning that, in certain situations, we will fight, run away or freeze in response to danger. The second is the limbic or mammalian brain, which is about motivation and memory, meaning we remember the situations or sensations that cause us to fight, flee or freeze. Third is the human brain involving the neocortex, which brings with it the ability to reason and communicate through language.

This gives us the ability to ask whether we need to run away from the situation.

REPTILIAN BRAIN	MAMMAL BRAIN	HUMAN BRAIN
Brain stem and cerebellum	Limbic system	Neocortex
Fight or flight	Emotions, memories, habits	Language, abstract thought, imagination, consciousness
Autopilot	Decisions	Reasons, rationalises

The amygdala: red-zone or green-zone bias

The amygdala is an almond-sized region in the brain, which acts as the emotional or memory centre. It sits at the base of the limbic brain, and it holds a library of learnt experiences, so we can react appropriately when we face similar situations in the future. It determines whether the reaction is fight, flee or freeze (red zone) or calm and be (green zone). It's there to protect us and ensure survival. It controls emotions and behaviours, as well as memory formation, and helps to regulate anxiety, aggression, fear conditioning, emotional memory and social cognition.

We know that when we breathe well the amygdala is calm and quiet, but when we are breathing poorly, it can run red hot. If we're breathing poorly and are faced with a perceived or real threatening situation or a scary childhood memory, this system is triggered. For example, if someone was physically abused as a child, the memory library in their amygdala may have a red flag surrounding a raised arm. Then, in later life, if that person is in the supermarket and another shopper lifts up their arm to reach over their head to pick something off a high shelf, the amygdala can override the rational brain, hijacking it to expect to be hit again. This is aptly called an amygdala hijack. There is no rational brain process involved in this reaction, which can cause the person to run or react unfavourably as their body is flooded with stress chemicals. This entire process is exacerbated if the amygdala is already red hot as a result of the person breathing poorly.

If the amygdala is calm and we're breathing well, our higher centres function optimally, so we can apply logic and reason: *I am not going to be hit. This person is reaching over my head for something.* Danger is diverted. When someone raises an arm towards you, this is not always an act of violence.

When you receive a text message and there's no smiley face in it, that does not mean the sender is angry, sad or anything else. That is just a story created in the mind.

Many of these responses are subconscious as they have been programmed, but with help, often from qualified health professionals, these triggers can be acknowledged, brought into our awareness and released, and our response then altered. Breathing well helps to uncover the hidden messages and helps change the response, but sometimes it's the body itself that keeps us in a tailspin.

Breathing well can help us to trump the emotional brain and enable us to access reason before we react.

Summary

Breathing well is a fundamental function, *not* an exercise. Breathing well empowers you to be well. Breathing well creates:

- energy efficiency of muscle use, saving precious oxygen for vital organs
- a strong pumping action which causes healthy pressure regulation.

Heart rate variability and a state known as resonance create the ultimate calm state. This is at five to seven breaths per minute.

Symptoms occur if CO_2 levels are too low, or too high, leading to scary symptoms that often cause fear and panic. Break the vicious cycle.

Over-breathing at rest drives carbon dioxide levels down resulting in:

- reduction in blood flow to the brain

- oxygen not being easily released to cells
- blood vessels constricting
- the nervous system moving us towards the sympathetic or red zone
- lactate in the muscles not being cleared efficiently
- stimulation of the nerve–muscle junction preparing the body to run
- mast cells releasing more histamine.

If we breathe well, we can access reason before reacting.

CHAPTER 3

SELF-CHECKING

Self-awareness and breathing well at rest

Breathing is not as simple as in and out. Each person has their own unique rhythm, style and pattern, and it's important that you physically connect with yours.

Awareness is 50 per cent of the way towards understanding what breathing well means. First, this includes knowing what healthy breathing is and, secondly, it involves physically feeling your breathing rhythm.

Awareness of the breath and paying attention to it can trigger the pathway towards the green zone and relaxation without altering anything else. I strongly encourage you to pause several times each day just to observe and follow your breath.

The first step towards breathing well is to tune into the breath and the body.

TRY THIS SELF-CHECK

While sitting, standing or even lying, place one hand on your chest with your index finger resting on your collarbone, and the other hand on your abdomen over your belly button.

Now feel your breathing, feel your pattern, and feel the movement.

Start with the breath in, called the inhale.

• Are you breathing in through your nose or your mouth?

• Is the air warm or cold?

• Does it feel easy or stuffy?

• Is one nostril working and the other not?

• Is your jaw clenched?

• Are your teeth touching?

As the breath travels down, feel the pattern and feel the movement.

• Which hand is moving first and most—your upper or lower hand?

• Is your chest moving? Does it move in or out on the in breath? Does it move in or out on the out breath?

• Is your abdomen moving? Does it move in or out on the in breath?

Does it move in or out on the out breath?

Just feel the breath.

Now count how many breaths you are taking in a minute. One breath is counted as breathing in and breathing out.

• Set the timer on your phone for three minutes.

• Count your breaths over the three minutes.

• Divide the number of breaths by three to work out your breaths per minute.

The rate per minute is an indicator of what may be happening at rest, and there are parameters in the medical field indicating what is within the expected norm, depending on age and development.

Note: If you are observing someone else and measuring their breath rate per minute, the key is not to tell them as breathing is both a conscious and unconscious function. When awareness is brought to the breath, we can alter it unknowingly.

Tune in and feel the following then tabulate your results. Recheck after three to six weeks of awareness and practice.

Rate per/min			

Circle your symptoms:

Pattern

Nose	Mouth
Lower hand moves most	Upper hand moves most
Pause at the end of in or out breath	No pause
Small, gentle breaths	Large, laboured breaths

Rhythm

Regular	Irregular
Smooth	Jerky
Rhythmical	Erratic

Sound

Quiet	Noisy
Soft	Hard
Regular	Stilted

Breathing well at rest

There is no one correct way to breathe. Each of us has our own unique pattern. We all vary in rate, volume and rhythm. However, there are ways of breathing that are more effective than others, and some general pattern characteristics we know are helpful.

Breath has a rate, pattern, sound, depth and energy requirement. Ideal rates per minute at rest are:

- babies—35–58 breaths
- toddlers—15–22 breaths
- adolescents—12–16 breaths
- adults—8–12 breaths (this is after the lungs stop growing at around 22 years of age)

When breathing well:

- the pattern is rhythmical and regular
- you move the air in and out through your nose into your belly
- as you breathe in, your belly rises, and as you breathe out, your belly falls
- the exhale is slightly longer than the inhale, with a gentle pause before taking in a new breath
- the sound is soft
- movement is effortless
- the volume is not big.

It's important to mention the volume of the air we breathe. Obviously, we cannot measure the volume ourselves, but it is often a lot less than we would expect. Breathing well means breathing low, slow and certainly not big.

Deep versus big

There's often confusion between big and deep breathing. Deep breathing is also referred to as diaphragmatic, belly or abdominal breathing. It involves breathing into the nose and belly, and—for the average adult—breathing at a volume of about 500 mL per breath (5L per minute), which is not a lot. Big breathing usually involves moving larger volumes of air into the upper chest.

It's important to understand the difference between deep and big breathing, as many people misinterpret the term 'deep' to mean 'big', so they start big breathing all the time, which is a disaster in the making. Big breathing at rest causes CO_2 levels to drop quickly and thereby trigger scary symptoms as the brain is told to panic.

At times, we need to take a full breath, which may also be called big, and there are three components to this big, full breath:

1. Breathe a low volume of air through the nose into the belly (deep breathing).

2. As demand increases, expand the ribcage sideways to pull in more air. The ribcage moves more to draw more air in during demanding situations, such as increased physical movement.

3. Finally, breathe upwards into the chest to pull in even more air, just like filling up an accordion. This is a full, big breath volume.

When you exercise or are highly stimulated, these large volumes and all three components of breathing are required as the body's chemistry changes to meet the demand for more oxygen to be delivered to power the cells. Many people breathe primarily using the upper chest all of the time. Instead, you should save upper-chest breathing for excitement, activity or effort, when you actually need more oxygen.

TRY THIS BODY SCAN

While seated or lying down:
Start at your feet.
• What do they feel like?
• Can you feel your toes, the soles of your feet, your ankles and feet?
Move up to your legs.
• Are they loose or tense?
• Try clenching them, then let go. They should roll out loosely.
Gently move your pelvis backwards and forwards and from side to side.
Clench your buttocks and release.
Is your gut loose and floppy or tight and tense?
Check your shoulders.
• Gently raise and release them, then pull back and drop them.
Check your hands.
• Stretch your fingers and thumbs, then release.
Check your jaw and tongue—this is very important.
• Are your teeth touching?
• Where is your tongue sitting in your mouth? Your tongue should sit gently behind your top teeth, and your

teeth should only touch when eating steak.

Wiggle your jaw, soften your lips and allow your tongue to rest behind your top teeth.
- Where is the tension?
- Where is it sore?

When you practise at rest, you'll know you are big breathing if you quickly begin to feel dizzy. Taking in the big volume of air when it's not necessary blows out your CO_2 balance and starts moving you towards the red zone.

Body tension

An absolute prerequisite to breathing awareness and retraining is to understand where you hold tension in your body. I cannot emphasise enough the importance of awareness of body tension. If any part of us is tense, this triggers a signal to the brain to move towards the red zone. As a result, our breathing will alter and a cycle will be created. If you recognise when and where your hot spots are, it will make the world of difference.

Jaw clenching deserves a mention here. Nearly all my clients who are deskbound come in with tight, tense jaws. The jaw tightens to protect our teeth when we are in danger. If the jaw is tense and tight, I can pretty much conclude that the person is in the red zone, alert to danger.

In the animal kingdom, tooth-sharpening behaviour, which is called thegosis, prepares animals for the threat of danger. Anyone from a farm knows the sound of sheep grinding their teeth when held in pens and are stressed. Anyone who works in live seafood export knows the clapping of lobsters' claws as they are boxed and become stressed when readied for export.

As for humans, dentists are now observing an increase in patients grinding their teeth as a result of living in the red zone. At the same time, it appears we have lost the art of chewing. We speed-eat, and this lack of chewing reduces muscle action of the jaw and tongue, which leads to poorly formed jaws and mouths.

The body language of stress

- The shoulders are raised
- The head moves forward
- The jaw is clenched
- The tongue tightens
- The fists are clenched
- The abdominal muscles tighten
- The buttock and thigh muscles tighten
- The legs are tense and often crossed
- The feet move or tap

Know your warning signs

- When you get tense, which parts of your body store the tension?
- Which part tenses first?
- What happens to your breathing in these situations?
- What are your warning signs and symptoms when you become fatigued?

It's worth finding out the answers to the above questions. They should not be taken lightly and should be respected as an ally.

Viv, 45, presented with daily headaches, persistent neck and shoulder pain, poor sleep and sensations of anxiety. She had a busy job and was on the go constantly. On examination, Viv was incredibly tense, which was affecting her breathing pattern. She had no idea of the tension she held in her body. Even when Viv was lying down, her legs were tight and tense.

The first step to treatment was for Viv to spend a week with an alarm set every 30 minutes to remind her to stop and let the tension in her legs go. After a week of this, she was already feeling better. This was just the start of her treatment, but this powerful self-awareness exercise gave her the tools to check and self-correct. As a result, she felt empowered to do something simple to improve how she was feeling.

UNDERSTAND YOUR BODY — LISTEN TO YOUR BODY		
· Calm · Relaxed · Present · Connected · Body-neutral	· Breathing discomfort · Frequent sighing and yawning · Short of breath for no reason · Problems with voice/speech · Headaches · Upset gut/nausea · Clammy hands · Chest pains · Dizzy spells or feeling spaced-out · Feeling of 'air hunger' · Erratic heartbeats · Achy muscles and joints	· Altered habits · Eating more/less · Drinking more · Smoking more · Increased absence · More accident-prone · Disturbed sleep · Feeling anxious and uptight · Shattered confidence · Tired all the time · Irritability or hyper-vigilance
Rest, Digest, Repair, Recover Breath: Nose, low, slow, rhythmical GREEN ZONE	**In between** Breath: Shallow, big, breath-holding, muscle tension	**Resilience, Danger, Fear, Anxiety** Breath: Shallow, fast, mouth, breath-holding, statue PROLONGED RED ZONE

Evidence-based research tells us it takes three to six weeks to change a habit. The table above lists some of the most common signs, symptoms and habits associated with the zones of the autonomic nervous system. Where do you currently sit—green zone, red zone or somewhere in between?

If the red zone is dominating and you have been there for some time, please take action by using the tools and techniques shared here to start the process towards self-awareness and empowerment over your health.

It still astounds me the number of people who don't know how to feel their muscle tension. In the Western world, we appear to avoid or have lost the ability to feel physically and, often, emotionally, instead tending to get caught up in our thoughts. The first step towards changing this is to stop and physically feel:

• our breathing patterns
• our physical tension.

We can then begin to listen to our bodies and fine-tune them accordingly.

Summary

• Breathing well is an individualised exercise.
• Breathing well at rest for an adult is at a rate between 8–12 breaths per minute, nose, low (abdomen), slow, quiet, rhythmical and effortless.
• It is very important not to confuse deep with big.
• Know your body stress.

- Know your warning signs.
- Listen to your body.

CHAPTER 4

IT'S RIGHT UNDER YOUR NOSE

The biomechanics of breathing

The body connection

Toby is 35 and he came to me because he was tired of waking up every morning feeling like he had been hit by a bus. He knew he needed to do something about it.

As Toby's breath was audible and strained, it was clear that he couldn't use his nose well. He had broken his nose several times during his rugby career, which had left him with a partially deviated septum that resulted in poor nasal airflow (patency). My recommendation was that he have nasal surgery then come back to me to relearn how to use his nose.

When asked about his experience, Toby said, 'Never underestimate the importance of the nose. Not until you have to do without it do you realise what a difference it makes. The ten days post-surgery were even worse than normal. I had to breathe a hundred per cent with my mouth. I had such a bad time—I couldn't smell, I couldn't taste food, my mouth was dry. Worst of all, my sleep was disturbed, and I had the most bizarre dreams. It was literally a nightmare.'

TRY THIS NASAL AIRFLOW SELF-ASSESSMENT EXERCISE

Air should flow between both nostrils. If it doesn't, it could be due to an obstruction, an allergy or just pure habit.

1. Hold a small mirror or an old stainless-steel knife under your nostrils and exhale with a little more force than normal. Condensation should appear, indicating the airflow. Is the amount of condensation coming from

each of the nostrils different? Which has more? Which has less?

2. Try lightly blocking across the opening of one nostril with a finger or your thumb while breathing, then block the other nostril. Which one is working? Which one is stuffier?

Try this excercise again in a few hours to see if this sensation of nostril patency (how open the nose is) changes.

Another way to assess nasal airflow is to use a sinus rinse bottle to check if the saline solution flows through the nostrils. If your nose is completely obstructed, no fluid will come through. With a partial obstruction, the solution may only trickle through.

The nose is incredible and I'm going to tell you why, but first it's time to find out how well you can use your nose.

When doing these exercises, you may have found a different sensation between the airflow in each nostril. This is normal as the nostrils alternate sides as they carry out different functions. One side is cleaning and clearing, while the other side allows airflow into the lungs. This alternation of sides also influences the firing of various parts of the brain. The left nostril synchronises to the right side of the brain and is believed to be linked with the parasympathetic system (green zone). The right side synchronises with the left side of the brain and is believed to be linked to the sympathetic system (the red zone). Clearly, we need good nasal health in both nostrils.

I'm fascinated by the benefits of nasal breathing and I'm always learning about it. For simplicity, I will highlight only the key functions of the nose.

The key nasal functions

It warms the air

Air needs to be at body temperature by the time it hits the lungs. Interestingly, nasal shapes have been determined by evolution and environment. For example, the long Anglo-Saxon nose, with its origins in cooler, drier countries, allows more time for warming and humidification of the air before hitting the lungs. Those who live nearer the equator have smaller, wider noses because they do not require as much humidification or warming before the air reaches the lungs.

It moistens the air

The membrane in the lungs where gas exchange occurs must be moist for this to happen, so the air being breathed in needs to be moist. Plus, the warm, humid air enables the small, hair-like projections in the airways known as cilia to move mucus, continually cleaning and clearing the lungs.

It filters out impurities such as dust, dirt, bacteria, viruses and pollen

This prevents harmful substances in the air from entering the lungs. The nose also:

- creates mucus, which moves in a continuous flow to protect us from infection.
- allows a sense of smell, linking the nose to experience and emotion. (I fondly remember the smell of fresh scones from my mother's kitchen,

so now when I smell a freshly baked scone I am immediately triggered to the memory of my mother.)

- directs airflow, which determines our physical endurance. For example, trainers used to clip the inside of the nostrils of racehorses to make them run faster. Nasal expander devices that help with patency are now widely available and are used by many athletes as well as to improve sleep.

- creates pressure differences between the nose and lungs. This pressure difference allows efficient gas exchange to occur and ensures oxygen is transported to the body. Mouth breathing has less resistance, creating less pressure and causing decreased efficiency in the exchange of gases.

- delivers drugs directly to the brain. The nasal lining, called the nasal mucosa, is rich in blood vessels. This and the olfactory (nasal) nerve bundles allow an easy pathway to deliver chemicals directly to the brain, hence some recreational and pharmaceutical drugs being administered nasally, so the hit to the brain comes fast and hard.

Production of nitric oxide

With respect to immune health, one of the most important functions of the nose is the production of a gas called nitric oxide (NO). This gas is produced in the nasal cavity and, when we nasally breathe, it is transported down into the airway and lungs. Its function is to:

- sterilise incoming air.
- maintain mucociliary clearance, where the cilia move continuously to assist in mucus cleaning and clearing. If the cilia are not working, mucus will pool and become infected.
- function as a messenger to open the airway, triggering blood flow and oxygen uptake.
- play a role in regulation of the immune system.
- provide antiviral and antibacterial properties.

BREATHING TEST

Try using your mouth to take a breath, then try using your nose.

When breathing through your nose, it might feel like you're breathing through a straw. This resistance is essential to set the correct pressures to ensure efficient gas exchange. It also allows an increased efficiency of 10 to 20 per cent in the uptake of oxygen.

During the COVID-19 outbreak, many medical practitioners emphasised the importance of nasal breathing, largely due to the key function NO plays in viral protection. Research is being done into the effectiveness of dosing medical staff with NO to improve their immunity prior to undertaking shifts on the frontline.

Increasing the production of nitric oxide

To increase the production of NO, I advise people to hum until their lips tingle, for up to five minutes a day. The resonance humming produces in the nasal chamber dumps up to 15 times the normal amount of NO into the nasal cavity, so I encourage you all to hum to your heart's content. It only takes five minutes a day to get that healthy protection, so hum on the way to work, hum in the shower, hum while you're cooking and teach your kids to hum. I encourage everyone to do this to increase their protection against bacteria and viruses.

The nose is certainly our first line of defence. For more information, you may wish to read *Breathing Matters,* a book dedicated to the nose, which I co-wrote with otolaryngologist and ear, nose and throat physician Jim Bartley.

The vocal folds: the top of the pressure systems

The vocal folds are part of the larynx, which help with important functions such as protection from choking, assisting with airflow and the production of sound (phonation).

The vocal folds open during inhalation and come together and close during swallowing and phonation. Clinically, it's not uncommon to see people who overuse the muscles in the larynx and, as a result, hold too much air in the lungs. This is referred to as reversible dynamic hyperinflation, and we need to teach these individuals to relax and allow proper airflow around the throat area. An extreme example of this can be seen in weightlifters. They brace the abdomen, fill the lungs with air, then hold that air in by blocking off the larynx, so their vocal folds come tightly together (adduction). The force created within the intra-abdominal and intrathoracic cavities acts to protect the spine. The grunt they often make is caused by air escaping through the vocal folds.

Breathing well also creates the foundation of voice. The pumping action of the diaphragm and pressure change within the cavity causes the air to hit the vocal folds, causing vibration on the out breath. This is how the voice is created. Other structures, such as the tongue, palate and nasal passages, are then responsible for modifying sound. Hence when the nose is blocked, the voice is altered. For more on this, see chapter 12.

The diaphragm: the vital pump

The diaphragm is an incredible muscle. While all of the others get a break due to being paralysed during REM sleep, the diaphragm is the only skeletal muscle that works 24/7. It should move, at a minimum, approximately 16,000 times in 24 hours, making it a powerhouse built for strength and endurance. The muscle literally cuts us in half, and running through it are the major vessels of the body: the vena cava, aorta, oesophagus and lymphatic duct.

The movements that occur during breathing influence how these vessels function. The lymphatic duct travels alongside the spine at the back of the thoracic cage. Movement is crucial for circulation, which regulates our immune system, so this is an especially important function.

A good breathing pattern helps move about 4–5 litres of lymph per day. With an irregular movement pattern, this fluid can become stagnant. It's estimated that about 16,500 litres of blood traverses the capillaries in 24 hours. The lower fibres of the diaphragm wrap around the oesophagus and help act as an anti-reflux barrier working as a sphincter.

It is known that people with gastro-oesophageal reflux disease (GORD), which is also known as acid reflux, have decreased breathing function. Diaphragm strengthening can assist with the strengthening of this sphincter action. (See section entitled "Muscle strengthening" for inspiratory muscle training.)

Jim is 52 and he has had problems with gastric reflux for over a year. Within a month of undertaking breathing awareness and inspiratory muscle training, his symptoms decreased significantly.

The liver, stomach, intestines, spleen, kidneys, pancreas and reproductive organs all lie below the diaphragm. When we breathe well, these organs have a rich blood supply. Plus, movement acts to massage these organs, ensuring they receive the oxygen and adequate nutrients they require to function in a healthy way. In upper-chest breathing, these organs lose this benefit and all functions are impaired.

When you consider the movement that occurs in the abdominal cavity when we breathe, it's no wonder the diaphragm has been labelled the 'vital pump'.

Kate is 42 and has had constant problems with her bowel and stomach since she was in her teens. Kate's problem was that she had learnt to hold in her abdomen. As a result, the diaphragm could not move downwards effectively, which resulted in her breathing into her upper chest.

Once she relaxed her abdomen and began to breathe well, Kate found these functions began to regulate themselves within a period of two weeks.

Obesity hypoventilation is on the rise. This is when excess weight on the belly and chest makes it hard for the chest to expand, the diaphragm to move and allow ventilation to occur. In obese individuals, the diaphragm has been seen to have fatty infiltration in the muscle tissue, which adds a double whammy of deconditioning and breathing problems.

The pelvic floor: the bottom of the container

The pelvic floor muscles form a sling that sits under the pelvis. They are involved in bladder, bowel and sexual function, and they help to hold the pelvic organs in the correct place, preventing prolapse.

The pelvic floor muscles also work with the diaphragm, abdominal and back muscles, contributing to stability around the trunk and pelvis. Any issue that affects one of these groups can have an impact on the others. Correct breathing therefore has a role in the function of all the pelvic organs.

We expect a lot from these muscles! They need to be strong enough to keep you continent, and flexible enough to allow you to empty the bladder and bowel when you are ready. They also need to be able to relax to allow entry into the pelvis e.g. for sexual activity or internal examinations.

There are two things that can go wrong with the pelvic floor muscles:

- They can be weak and lengthened, causing issues such as leakage from the bladder or bowel, prolapse, erectile dysfunction.
- They can be overactive or tight, causing problems such as pain with sex, constipation, pelvic and genital pain, or urinary urgency. Overactive pelvic floor muscles are often associated with anxiety and faulty breathing patterns.

There are resources at the end of the book with information on how to carry out pelvic floor exercises and strengthen these muscles. However, if you already have symptoms, or if you're not quite sure that you can contract your pelvic floor correctly, I recommend you see a pelvic health physiotherapist. Look for somebody who as extra skills and training in this area, who is able to carry out a specific pelvic floor examination.

Twenty-nine-year-old Phoebe had found intercourse painful since the birth of her child. Phoebe is a high achiever and prior to the birth of her child she was an athlete. When she came to see me, she was also struggling with her body image and change of routine. She was tired and tense. She also held her gut in as a way of trying to attain her pre-baby body image. I soon ascertained that she was mouth breathing due to a stuffy nose as well as upper-chest breathing with a shallow pattern of 16 breaths per minute.

Her treatment involved nasal hygiene (see section entitled "Nasal rinsing"), breathing re-education with an emphasis on body scans and daily prompts to stop, drop and flop, as well as a pelvic breathing exercise (see section entitled "PELVIC BREATHING EXERCISE"). It is still a battle for Phoebe, but at least she can recognise when she is tense and now has pain-free intercourse.

Putting it all together

When we breathe in, the diaphragm action draws air in through the nose, past the open vocal folds and into the lungs. The diaphragm, which moves downwards, works in conjunction with the abdominal muscles, the deep back muscles and the pelvic floor muscles. The abdomen moves out a little, the pelvic floor lowers a little and the back arches a little, so flexibility is necessary. The reverse happens on the out breath.

This rhythm and movement is healthy and normal. The internal pressure in the chest and abdomen is important for core strength and stability, so all of these muscles need to be strong and co-ordinated, with the diaphragm orchestrating this.

Bracing postures and movements will affect the way we breathe, just as dysfunctional breathing will affect our movements and postures. Holding in the abdominal muscles too much is a common presentation. When we are standing, the deep abdominal muscles should only work at three to five per cent of their maximum strength; so just turned on enough to keep the pelvis in a good position; and when we are lying down the abdominal muscles should be totally relaxed, so let the belly go.

a.   Ideal movement in standing is when the intra-abdominal muscles work well together, so when we breathe in, the diaphragm moves down pulling air into the oxygen-rich, deep lobes of the lung. The back muscles, deep abdominal muscles, and the pelvic floor muscles work in synchronisation with the belly moving out and the pelvic floor moving down and the back moving in. This allows the correct pressure to be created for efficient gas exchange in the lungs and the muscles working in a co-ordinated, efficient motor pattern to contain the abdominal and pelvic contents. Note: This is when there is no load applied, such as lifting. When this occurs the pelvic floor is thought to contract and gently move up to help protect the pelvic organs and create more pressure, protecting the spine and gut contents as helping well as bladder control.

b. If the abdominal muscles are too tense when we breathe in, the belly cannot move outwards as it should. This often drives pressure upwards instead of outwards, causing poor pressure changes for the lungs, and overuse of muscles that shouldn't be working, among other things.

During forced exhalation (breathing out), such as when coughing, the abdominal muscles contract and force the relaxing diaphragm upwards. If the pelvic floor muscles are not functioning correctly, pressure will be placed on these muscles and can often cause continence issues and leakage of urine.

But if during forced exhalation and coughing, the pelvic floor muscles and deep abdominal muscles co-contract to protect the pelvic floor against descent and the lower abdominal wall from bulging out, this can help with incontinence issues.

Pelvic floor health is another specialist field of practice within physiotherapy. Should you have a problem, I suggest you search your local physiotherapy society and look for specialist women's health, or pelvic health physiotherapists.

Summary

The nose:
- warms and moistens the air
- filters out impurities such as dust, dirt, bacteria, viruses and pollen
- creates mucus
- allows a sense of smell, linking the nose to experience and emotion
- sterilises incoming air and has an antiviral and antibacterial function
- maintains mucociliary clearance
- improves immunity via the production of nitric oxide (NO)
- creates pressure differences between the nose and lungs.

Nasal breathing assists oral development and health.

The key functions of the vocal folds are:
- protection
- assisting with airflow
- production of sound.

The diaphragm:

- is built for endurance, as we breathe at least 18,000 times a day
- is run through by the major vessels: the vena cava, aorta, oesophagus and lymphatic duct
- massages all organs when it moves
- creates pressure for movement and posture
- creates airflow for the voice.

The pelvic floor:

- muscles support our bladder, uterus, rectum and important abdominal organs against gravity and any added downward pressure
- assists with pressure within the intra-abdominal cavity.

CHAPTER 5

LISTEN TO YOUR BODY, LISTEN TO YOUR MIND

Put the body, the breathing and the thinking mind together

The key to healthy functioning is balance. I've already introduced the concepts of the red and green zones—the physiological switchboard between calm and chaos—the amygdala, the memory library that stores information from birth, and which plays a role in how we react to emotional situations, plus the body's mechanical balancing act, including the pressure canisters within our bodies. But, in the twenty-first century, we cannot forget the thinking mind.

It took me some time to understand the concept of the thinking mind. I remember distinctly the moment I fully understood what it was and how to distance myself from it. I was on a mindfulness/meditation instructors' course in Australia and had just finished a meditation in a group when one of the members, a Buddhist monk, said, 'Wow! My mind was crazy during that meditation.'

Confused, I asked what he meant. He explained that our thoughts and thinking mind are just theories, ideas, words, sentences and images, which are spun out of either our memory library, or conscious and unconscious thought.

The skill to observe these thoughts, and to detach ourselves from the thinking mind, is a key concept to mindfulness, meditation and, I would say, general sanity.

To highlight the breath connection and our thinking mind, I liked the exercise in which a group of students was divided into two groups. One group practised relaxed, calm breathing, while the other undertook erratic mouth breathing. The students were then asked to write down what they were thinking.

Apparently, the erratic mouth breathers wrote down thoughts that resembled something out of a Stephen King horror novel, while the nose breathers wrote thoughts that were more rational and calm. This highlighted the effect breathing has on how and what we think. Erratic breathing paved the way for horror, while effortless breathing led to more controlled thoughts.

Mindfulness and meditation play a key role in achieving balance and taming the thinking mind. However, one thing I know is that unless we are in the green zone, it's impossible to observe our thoughts. Breathing well is the key to being in the green zone.

Breathing well is the precursor to mindfulness or meditation. In fact, it is the precursor to most things.

The practice of mindfulness has swept the Western world over the past decade. This is great, as we need to pay attention to our mind and body. In the Western world, we often live in our thoughts and minds.

According to the American mindfulness and meditation expert Jon

Kabat-Zinn, mindfulness means paying attention on purpose, in the present moment and in a non-judgmental way. In essence, it is the practice of being present.

Meditation, which means 'to ponder', has been around for thousands of years, but in the past few decades Western researchers have begun to test the effects of meditation and to learn about its numerous benefits.

It is a process, a journey of discovery, that has steps in its learning. The initial step is the practice of mindfulness. The next steps in the meditation journey are intention, and then inquiry-type meditations.

Intention = affirmations via imagery, loving kindness and gratitude.

Inquiry = contemplation, who am I? This is a deeper, tougher practice.

If you're not breathing well, the benefits of practices such as yoga, meditation and mindfulness will not be as great.

This reminds me of another experience during the same training course. One of the other attendees kept saying 'I just don't get it', 'I can't feel it', 'It's just not happening for me'.

After day four, the instructors realised she had a dysfunctional breathing pattern, so they asked if I could do some work with her. She was what we call a 'fab ab' holder, meaning she held her belly tightly clenched and she had a big upper-chest breathing pattern.

Following some body work and breathing exercises (learning how to breathe well), she was able to *feel* what the instructors had been talking about, she calmed down and finally achieved the ability to observe her thoughts.

Mindfulness and meditation are great practices. The same goes for yoga and many other physical forms of movement, but please learn or know how to breathe well before you undertake any of these. The breath is the foundation for all of these practices, and if you're not breathing well, the benefits of such practices will not be as great.

A MINDFULNESS EXERCISE

- Start with a quick body scan (see box entitled "TRY THIS BODY SCAN") and follow your breath for several breaths.
- Then become aware of the following sensations.
- What can you hear inside and outside of the space you are in? Follow your breath.
- What can you smell? Follow your breath.
- Focus on your feet and/or hands.
- Again, follow your breath.

The first step to observe the thinking mind is through body and breath awareness. It is as simple as that.

The attention brought to the senses of sound and smell, and physical awareness of feet, hands and breath, are known as anchors. These anchors serve to focus attention away from the thinking mind and draw attention to the present moment.

With practice, and the choice of which anchor works best for you—breath, sound, smell, or physical sensations—this can be incorporated into your day easily in order to break the mind fix and constant dialogue that may not be serving you well.

The realisation that the thinking mind is only one part of us, often a part we have allowed to dominate and that we can tame, is profound.

Panic episodes: panic attacks

Panic deserves a heading in neon, because initial panic episodes are often caused by acute over-breathing, which is known as hyperventilating. In the future, the fear of these symptoms can further cause us to panic. Often the association of the episode surrounding the first attack can trigger subsequent attacks or condition us to anticipate panic attacks.

The physicality of a panic attack is often the aspect that affects people most. They remember and fear this and will often associate the first place they had an attack with that fear. For example, I had a client who experienced panic sensations in the shower. He was a shocking breather and the humidity of the steam led to him breathing harder. This was enough to tip the scales into the red zone, triggering panic feelings. By the time he came to see me he was experiencing panic in the hallway before he even reached the bathroom or turned on the shower.

Flying is a common trigger for panic. Modern aeroplanes still have an altitude pressure factor in the cabin that drives us to change how we breathe. When we mix breathing poorly with a few other factors such as skipping breakfast causing low blood sugar, drinking alcohol, the hot, humid temperature on the plane, and talking a lot and fast, then—Wham!—a stress bomb resulting in a panic attack.

As CO_2 is driven to very low levels, the sensation then becomes attached to the situation instead of the body chemistry. The brain then looks for a reason for the fear, so the mind will often create a fantastic story like 'The plane is going to crash' or 'I'm going to die!'. Thus, the cycle is set.

These triggers can be either at a conscious or an unconscious level.

Recent research has shown that the body will give significant warning signals an hour prior to a panic episode. I teach individuals how to listen to and feel these signals or, better still how to stop the trigger in the first place.

See chapter 3 for the identification of symptoms and understanding which zone you are in. See also the 'Break the vicious cycle' graph on above pages.

What drives a panic episode?

Panic cannot occur unless CO_2 in the body is either too low or too high. It's not just thought or misinterpretation of symptoms that drives carbon dioxide—many other things do too. We know what happens when CO_2 drops and what factors contribute to driving CO_2 down in order to help regulate panic and anxiety (see chapter 2).

BRADCLIFF BREATHING CALM-DOWN, BLISS-OUT EXERCISE: FOR A QUIET BODY AND A QUIET MIND

This is a quick exercise of body awareness and the breath. It takes about two minutes and can easily be done anywhere, so do it often.

Preparation

- Locate a quiet place.
- Perform a full body stretch.
- Sit comfortably on a chair.
- Plant your feet firmly on the floor.
- Either cup your hands in your lap or place them palms down on your lap.
- Make sure that your bottom is right against the back of the chair.
- Relax your stomach and loosen your shoulders while maintaining an open, upright posture.

Body awareness

To help you relax tensed muscles and focus on your breathing:

- Tuck your chin in, hold for five seconds and release.
- Drop your jaw for three seconds, then release and close your mouth, softly resting your tongue behind your top teeth.

- Lift your shoulders, then drop them, pull your shoulder blades together and down, and release.
- Stretch the fingers of one hand and then the other.
- Separate your fingers and stretch hard, especially the thumb.
- Rock your pelvis backwards and forwards, side to side, then relax somewhere in between.
- Loosen your legs and let them rest.
- Feel your feet on the ground.

Breathing

To draw your attention to the breath:

- Focus on the quiet breath, in and out through the nose.
- Feel your belly and waist expand gently, breathing in and flowing into the out-breath phase.
- Do not hold at the peak of inhalation, but notice the small, relaxed pause at the end of the exhale. Do not hold, just let go.

Quiet mind

To still your busy brain:

- Concentrate on silently counting numbers during the relaxed pause phase.
- This can be done with the eyes closed, or with the eyes open.
- Focus on a particular object, then soften the eyes (stop hard focusing).
- Do not try to stop thoughts, simply concentrate on the rhythmic flow of numbers.
- Start the numbering at one and move up to 10, then back down to one.
- Breathe in ... breathe out ... let go ... ONE
- Breathe in ... breathe out ... let go ... TWO
- Breathe in ... breathe out ... let go ... THREE (and so on to 10 then back down to one again).
- When you come back to one, stretch, smile and enjoy the calm.

If thoughts are persistent, that is OK. Just notice them, then return to focusing on your breath and the counting, or focus on your feet on the floor.

It may even help to pay attention to sounds both inside and outside the room. These anchors help to bring you back to the present moment.

Learn to use this exercise in times of mental or emotional overload in order to help calm your system and gain insight into what is going on for you.

Triggers that can exacerbate acute attacks

Heat and humidity

Most people find humid conditions muggy and airless, but for bad breathers this sensation is worse as the air is more dense. We all breathe harder in a humid situation, but a bad breather will breathe even more, thereby triggering symptoms and moving them into the red zone. This is why many bad breathers do not like enclosed spaces, or hot stuffy rooms. It's also why they want to have open windows and moving air. I always suggest to my dysfunctional breathers that they carry a hand fan. I also encourage all patients with lung disease to use moving air when they experience the sensation of breathlessness. Moving air triggers a nerve called the trigeminal nerve to decrease the sensation of breathlessness.

Rest

Rest can make things worse. If the dysfunctional breathing pattern is chronic, respiratory control centres are permanently reset. This new set point is low on carbon dioxide, so when we rest by going to bed, watching TV or going on holiday, the body slows breathing and the carbon dioxide starts to increase. The brain chemistry is not used to this increase, so it sets off an alarm to breathe more as something is wrong.

This is one explanation for the initial air hunger experienced with breathing retraining. As new normals are set, the body will react. It takes time to readjust back to what is considered a healthy breathing pattern.

Blood glucose changes

During over-breathing, blood glucose concentration at the lower limit of the normal range decreases brain activity to a level normally associated with coma or sleep. So, if your blood glucose is low when you over-breathe, you are more likely to get symptoms. Conversely, if blood glucose levels are normal, you are less likely to get symptoms when you over-breathe. This is discussed more fully in chapter 9.

Voice use

Some people lower their blood CO_2 levels when they speak. These are people who often speak rapidly, breathing fast and predominantly in their upper chests. They literally draw little breath.

Menstruation

Blood CO_2 levels go down in the second half of the menstrual cycle as progesterone is released. Progesterone is known as a respiratory stimulant. So premenstrually or during ovulation a dysfunctional breather will often have worse symptoms.

Stimulants

The role of stimulants, such as caffeine, is discussed more fully in chapter 9, but these will all drive the over-breather towards the red zone. These chemicals are known panicogens, which is a chemical that triggers panic. Carbon dioxide is one of the best-known panicogens, so when someone with low CO_2 tolerance is exposed to any of the triggers that drive CO_2 down, it can quickly set off the panic/anxiety alarm.

Extreme exercise

People who do extreme sports such as sky diving often activate the fight or flight response. Their limbic systems can cause them to hyperventilate or over-breathe.

Poor posture and physical limitations due to tight clothing

Poor posture and tight clothing can affect breathing patterns.

Note: These triggers, which all drive CO_2 lower, may also provoke symptoms but not always result in an attack. They may be present alone or in combinations that accumulate and finally tip the scales into panic.

Triggers can either trip you or make you more susceptible to panic episodes, especially if you have had recent episodes, or you are tired or stressed.

When you are tired, you tend to hyperventilate, and this activates the sympathetic nervous system (red zone). Uncontrolled stress also activates similar pathways.

First-year university student Joseph was experiencing panic episodes that were beginning to interfere with his life. As a result, he avoided social gatherings in the fear that someone would notice how anxious he was or that he might have an attack in public. Little did he realise that people cannot usually see a panic attack, even though it feels scary as it is a massive stress bomb. Joseph admitted these sensations started after he took some party pills, then eventually increased until it was a daily living nightmare. Thankfully, he stopped drinking alcohol and taking the pills or any other stimulants during this time. But his nervous system had gone crazy.

Medication often helps in this situation, so it does pay to see your GP.

Luckily for Joseph, we equipped him with the tools to help return him to the green zone. (See chapter 8 for the breathing basics.) Plus, the Five by Fives exercise (see box entitled "BRADCLIFF FIVE BY FIVES BREATHING EXERCISE FOR RECOVERY") for recovery breathing was an essential exercise for Joseph to use as soon as he felt symptoms. Education was also important so Joseph could understand what was triggering his symptoms.

When you feel symptoms occurring, try the following:

- Focus on exhaling—pursed-lipped exhaling can help. Breathe in and out of your nose where possible to help you to gain control.
- Check your body tension and try to loosen up. You may need to stand and move or adopt relaxed breathing postures, such as arms behind your back or above your head, resting forward onto a table.

These can be used to manage a panic attack or episodes of breathlessness. (For relaxed postures, see section entitled "Other things that can help".)

- Repeat self-affirmations such as 'Breathe in and out' and 'Let go'.
- Talk to yourself—'This has happened before so I know it will pass.'
- Try to put things into perspective—is it really that bad?
- Think of your feet—grounding can be helpful. (See the grounding exercise in section entitled "EXERCISES AND OTHER STRATEGIES".)
- Moving air helps, so use a hand fan, open a window or go outside.

Summary

- Breathing well is the precursor to mindfulness or meditation.
- The thinking mind can trick us.
- Learn how to be present in your body.
- Know what can trigger panic sensations and panic attacks.

- Use the BradCliff Five by Fives for recovery breathing.

BRADCLIFF FIVE BY FIVES BREATHING EXERCISE FOR RECOVERY

This is especially useful for recovery breathing during an acute panic episode.

1. Cup both hands over your nose and mouth and ensure they are tight.

2. Breathe softly in and out through the nose five times. This enables you to rebreathe the exhaled CO_2, raising your levels and helping to reduce symptoms.

3. Drop your hands to your lap and count up to five.

4. Breathing with cupped hands, repeat counting each breath in and out up to five.

5. Repeat this five by five sequence until the symptoms subside.

If panic continues, call someone you can talk to so you can get it off your chest. Cognitive therapy might also help.

Once the episode has passed, try to rest. A panic episode is exhausting and your body needs to recover. For next time, be aware of your triggers and slowly work through them.

In the past, people were handed paper bags to breathe into to restore CO_2 levels. This has fallen out of favour as it encourages people to overbreathe more. (The only time you're likely to see it now is in TV sitcoms or comedies.)

CHAPTER 6

THE STRESS CONNECTION

In the Western world, we eat stress. We live in the red zone, we set goals like there is no tomorrow, and we jump and scramble to get to the top. Life is about individualism and perfectionism instead of inclusivism and holism.

Those terrible twins stress and fatigue are a norm in our society, and the anxiety epidemic is growing at a significant rate. In 2020, the WHO reported that one in 13 people globally suffer from anxiety. In the United States, anxiety disorders are the most common mental illness, affecting 18.1 per cent of the population every year—and that was pre-COVID.

Stress is any demand that is placed upon us. Whether it's internal or external, mental or physical, positive or negative, stress is a normal, healthy and essential part of life. Stress is a normal physiological experience. We need it. Without stress, we would not get out of bed, we would not grow, and we would not develop resilience. However, stress becomes an issue when we experience too much of it for too long.

The way we breathe, as seen already, affects the autonomic nervous system, green zone, red zone. It also affects a key relaxation nerve, called the vagus nerve. This nerve acts like a handbrake on the sympathetic branch, the red zone, stopping it from firing. This is why, more than ever in our stress-hungry society, awareness of breathing and the influence it has is essential. Many of us live in a prolonged state of stimulation, ultimately resulting in inflammation of the body, and fatigue and exhaustion with adrenal burnout. If we breathe well, the vagus nerve is in top form, helping to reduce anxiety, to stablilise blood pressure and to keep us balanced.

Understanding our perception of stress

The key is for us to understand our individual perception of stress and how we react to the demands, pressures and challenges that are placed upon us.

Step one: Understanding the nervous system

The first step involves understanding the nervous system and listening to your body, knowing when you are in the red zone, the green zone or in the middle, then adjusting accordingly. If too much time is spent in either zone, we do not grow. Too long in the green zone and we will experience boredom, inertia and tedium. Too long in the red zone and we're at risk of burnout, overwhelm, depression and anxiety. Recheck the table in section entitled "Know your warning signs": where are you? Do you have healthy movement between both?

Step two: Understanding the language of stress

The second step is to learn to understand your language of stress, by which I mean learning to analyse what stress means for you.

'I'm so stressed.' 'I have too much stress.' 'I have anxiety.' 'I am so anxious.' 'I'm tired all the time.' 'I can't cope.' 'I can't breathe.' 'I am overwhelmed.' These are all statements I frequently hear from clients, so it's clear to me that stress is a suitcase word that needs to be unpacked.

There is a difference between all of the expressions used above to describe stress, and it's helpful to understand the difference so you can articulate your experiences when speaking to health professionals. The clearer you can be, the more targeted and effective the treatment will be.

Stress

Stress is any pressure placed upon us. It may be positive or negative, external or internal.

Anxiety

A feeling of fear or worry about what's to come in the future, a future projection. A psychologist once told me that anxiety is worry about the future while depression is rumination about the past.

Overwhelm

When we are overwhelmed, we are completely submerged by the thoughts and emotions surrounding a situation or event.

Panic attack

This is a sudden, intense sensation, almost like having an adrenaline shot. When you experience a panic attack, you are shot up with adrenaline. This massive surge of stress chemicals will be intense and will pass quickly as the chemicals subside. When this happens, you are left feeling exhausted. Panic and breathing are co-dependent; you cannot panic if you are breathing well—it is impossible.

Step three: Understanding the feeling of stress

The third step is to ask yourself where and how you feel stress, anxiety or panic. Where do you feel it? What does it feel like? When does it appear? Pain—sharp, dull, throbbing—can you name it?

Try to describe how your stress, anxiety and panic feel. Our emotional feeling centre runs along the centre of the body, so emotions will commonly be felt in the throat, heart, chest, upper gut or lower gut. These areas house significant nerve bundles called nerve plexuses, so from an anatomical point of view it makes sense that this is where overload is experienced.

Taming the thinking mind

One of my biggest concerns is the number of children and adolescents I hear saying, 'I have anxiety.' For a start, no one *has* anxiety, instead we *feel* anxious. Anxiety is a feeling associated with a thought or worry about something in the future, something that has not yet happened.

This is where taming the thinking mind and knowing what pushes us into the red zone and what triggers lower CO_2 help to educate us about what anxiety really is while also equipping us to deal with it.

As I say to all my clients who present with heaps of anxious feelings, you should become a fiction writer. These things have not happened yet, but you are creating a wonderful story around the potential of what may happen.

Sophie was a new graduate, who was applying for jobs. She was stuck in her thinking mind—'What if they don't like me?' 'Am I qualified enough?' 'I feel like I know nothing' 'I won't get the job'—and her body language and breathing pattern reflected this. She presented looking pale, frail and tense. She was nearly passing out with anxiety and fear.

I explained to her that her body didn't know that the things she feared weren't actually happening to her, so it was responding as if the things were happening in real time. I encouraged her to stop creating stories in her head, and instead to stick to the current chapter, which is here today, instead of skipping ahead. We worked on breathing for sleep and anxious feelings, and followed with breathing re-learning (see chapter 8).

After a week, Sophie was calmer but still anxious. After three weeks, she bounced in, feet on the ground, calmer and with the ability to stop and check what she was thinking. She was even laughing as she couldn't believe the stories she'd been telling herself and how bound up she had become in her own fictional belief system.

For Sophie, the education surrounding CO_2 dropping (see section entitled "Low blood levels of CO_2") was important, as she'd noticed her 'anxiety' was worse when she hadn't eaten, around the time of menstruation or if she wore tight jeans.

Technology triggers

For many people, using a computer may be a trigger to send them into the red zone, even though it is not a life-threatening situation. When this happens, we need to stop, respond, review and rest our body/brain. Many of us are permanently in the red zone when using electronics as a result of poor posture and dysfunctional breathing habits. Tight, tense muscles and breath-holding send the message to our brain that we are in danger. As a result, our body chemistry alters by moving us into the red zone, so chemicals are released, and we start to feel anxious. This is a physical trigger.

Breathing as a trigger

Oliver experienced anxiety sensations in his early teens, but he adopted excellent skills for self-management: yoga, relaxation, exercise, awareness of triggers and a healthy diet. The only problem was that he had implemented a breathing regime that involved big breaths as he had misinterpreted deep for big. In each stressful situation, he responded with big breaths, hoping for calm. However, those big breaths kept pushing his CO_2 levels lower and tipping him into more anxiety, panic and overwhelm. This set up a vicious cycle that even the best counsellor and medication could not shake.

It wasn't until a deep, nose, low and slow, effortless and natural breathing pattern was restored that he started to feel what true calm was and his symptoms began to settle. He also realised the gym work he had been doing was further tightening the chest muscles, which left his emergency breathing muscles working too much.

Over time, Oliver began to listen to his body and respond by breathing well. He was then able to create a distance between emotion and reaction. This breathing space gave him the ability to acknowledge that no one could actually make him feel anything—the feeling comes from a response to the *emotion. Breathing well brought his power and control back.*

Our breathing is the body's way of signalling distress. It is one of the first and most visible signs. Emotion is felt, the memory library searches for a meaning, then we have feelings associated and behaviour or a response occurs. There are many triggers, involving physical, emotional and environmental factors. The breath is a key to help understand our response and reaction, and then to help alter the response and reaction in a way that bridges the gap between emotion, thought and feeling. Don't get me wrong, this is not easy. Breathing well is a simple concept but takes time, practice and awareness.

Breathing dysfunction is often prevalent in Type A achievers, usually because they push, push, push. Perceived threat and red-zone dwelling sends a message to the brain: 'I am in danger!' Being able to recognise this and knowing how to pull back from it helps us to maintain balance.

The three steps to treat stress

Step 1: Feel and express what your body is telling you

The first step in understanding stress is to feel what is happening as emotion presents physically in your body. This starts to marry together the mind–body concept. Our physical feelings can be an indicator of what is going on for us emotionally.

Culturally, we are not great at feeling or understanding our emotions. Many of us have been conditioned to suppress how we feel—boys don't cry, girls don't fly into a rage. When you hold back tears or stifle anger during a charged confrontation, or tiptoe on eggshells or ignore trauma unconsciously, you might hold your breath or change your breathing.

'Suck it up' and 'Pull yourself together' are sayings that are used commonly and often unwisely. I wonder if this is part of the problem that we are seeing in many of our teenagers, who are unable to untangle and understand their emotions.

We know that emotional expression leads to well-being, while suppression of emotions can lead to physical stress on the body.

The graph in section entitled "Step 1: Feel and express what your body is telling you" by British clinical psychologist Ashley Conway outlines the outcomes of emotional expression as opposed to emotional suppression. I refer to it often, as it highlights how important it is to honour the emotion. This does not have to be a verbal expression. It might be time spent quietly listening and realising 'I feel sad' or 'I feel angry'.

Sit with the emotion and it will pass. Expressing an unpleasant emotion, such as anger or fear, can be done in a way that doesn't hurt or threaten others—instead it can improve communication and connection. This is a real skill, and some of us have experienced it done really badly. It's possible to learn how to express unpleasant emotions well by researching and reading about this or by seeing an appropriate professional.

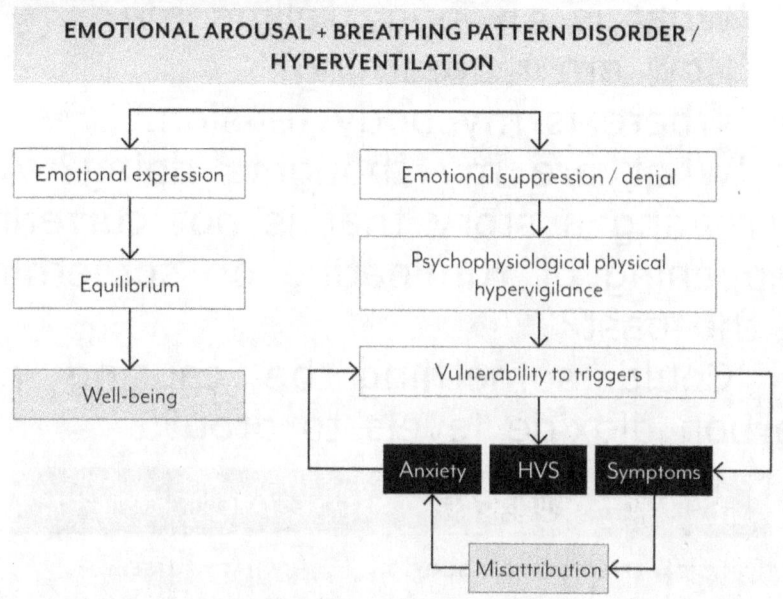

EMOTIONAL AROUSAL + BREATHING PATTERN DISORDER / HYPERVENTILATION

What are your signals and symptoms?

The table in section entitled "What are your signals and symptoms?" shows the physical effects of being in the red zone and their corresponding physical sensations.

To find out what your signals and symptoms are, pause, breathe, then listen/feel your body, and ask the question 'What is going on?' The answer is there should you dare to look.

Other factors that feed anxiety and stress sensations may be purely chemical drivers that lower CO_2, so it is important to stop, feel, ask and listen:

'What is my body telling me?'

'How am I breathing?'

'Where is my body tension?'

'What are my thoughts doing? Am I creating a story that is not currently happening or ruminating on something in the past?'

'Could something be causing my carbon dioxide levels to drop?'

THE EFFECTS OF BEING IN A CONSTANT STATE OF 'RED ALERT'	
PHYSICAL EFFECTS ON THE BODY	WHAT YOU FEEL
· Breathing rates change · Upper-chest breathing becomes a habit · Blood flow is redirected to the arms and legs ('flight, do battle' muscles) · Blood flow is diverted away from the stomach · Adrenaline and cortisol levels rise, heart rate increases · Fluctuations in blood pressure · Increase in body temperature · Reduced saliva production · Sleep disturbances	· Sighing, yawning, 'air hunger' · Chronic tiredness, chest/neck/jaw pain, poor concentration · Physical tenseness and tremor in arms and legs, achy muscles · Nausea, reflux, ulcers · Palpitations, hypervigilance, suppressed immune system · Headaches, light-headedness · Increase in sweating · Dry mouth · Tired, fatigued

By simply paying attention to the way we breathe, even without adjusting it, we can begin to calm our bodies and settle our thoughts. The brain is soothed by the predictability of the inhale following exhale, following the inhale, following the exhale, even if the breath isn't exactly smooth and calm. However, in an acute situation, the first step is always the BradCliff Five by Fives.

Step 2: Identify your triggers

There are numerous triggers that can lower CO_2 drivers, which can ultimately cause you to feel anxiety, stress, overwhelm or panic, as seen below. All of these can cause a panic attack or symptoms, especially if you have a disordered breathing pattern, or have had recent episodes of hyperventilation, or you are overtired or stressed. The triggers can occur in isolation or several at a time. If you're consistently exposed to these triggers, it is possible to end up in a state of chronic anxiety.

Take a second now to reflect upon what your triggers might be. When do you get symptoms? Do you need more than one trigger to be present before symptoms kick in?

SOME COMMON TRIGGERS

- Heat and humidity.
- Rest—if 'bad breathing' is chronic, the respiratory control centres are reset. When rest is needed—for example, when going to bed, watching TV or going on holiday—the body loses the ability to relax fully, and when we try to, it is almost as if an alarm goes off and sends us into a panic state.
- Decreased blood glucose as a result of skipping meals.
- A lot of fast, continuous talking or prolonged laughter can make you feel light-headed. Even though this is just the result of your CO_2 dropping, it can still feel scary.
- Stimulants such as caffeine and sugar.
- Menstruation, especially during the premenstrual week and the early days of the period.
- Extreme exercise.
- Poor posture.

- Physical restrictions due to tight clothing, like belts or bras.
- Fluorescent lights. When the light hits the retina, this sends a message to speed up breathing, so the effect is the same as that of a strobe light.
- Other emotional triggers, such as grief or fear.

Step 3: Implement stress-busting strategies

The third step is to act by implementing strategies to prevent stress. (See chapter 8 as breathing well is essential for calm.)

Stop, pause, feel and breathe, and widen the gap between a reaction and a response. (See section entitled "Summary" in chapter 6.) This allows a nanosecond for the rational brain to assess whether you really are in danger or not, and then it can scan the body and figure out what it needs. Slow the system, and allow the frontal cortex to re-engage to allow rationality and reason.

Breathing well allows for insight, feeling and a measured response. It is the most important tool we equip people with. Start simply by using the BradCliff green dot respond reset exercise.

BRADCLIFF GREEN DOT RESPOND RESET EXERCISE

Place green dots in strategic places. For example, on your computer, cell phone, the dashboard of your car, on the fridge and on doorways. Use these dots as a visual cue to remind yourself to stop and breathe out. When you do this, focus on the exhale, then follow with a nose belly breath.

Aim to do this a couple of times an hour. Alternatively, you could set an hourly reminder on your phone.

BradCliff stop, drop and flop

Stop—breathe out and feel your chest relax Drop—your shoulders down (check this often, hourly if possible) Flop—relax all over and breathe low and slow

Pause, breathe, respond, reset

The simple act of taking a breath, exhaling and allowing a pause can make a massive difference in how we react to a situation as it pulls us into the green zone.

The diagram in section entitled "Summary" in chapter 6 highlights what happens when we prolong the exhale or just pause and breathe. This allows a nanosecond longer, so the brain can process more efficiently what is going on. It also allows time for an appropriate response to a real or perceived threat.

During the COVID-19 lockdowns, I had Zoom meetings with several CEOs who were under the pump. Pressure was extremely high for many of them, so they spent a lot of their time making phone calls and talking. One of them told me that he was continually talking on the phone with no break, call after call after call. As a result, by the afternoon, he was so tense and tired, he just couldn't catch his breath when he was speaking. This led to him becoming short-fused.

All we did was implement this simple exercise—between each call, he would stop, focus on a breath out, try to stretch, pause and then make the next call. Where possible, he also implemented the two-minute, calm-down, bliss-out exercise (see section entitled "What drives a panic episode?"). This helped and although the pressure was still there, he was able to manage it better.

Five mini stress-busters

This is a quick-fire way to stop the chaos.

1. Pause

Stop, take a mini break ... hourly ... often.

2. Change

Change what you are doing—a problem is never solved from the same state in which it was created.

3. Stretch

Physical movement unlocks the body and hence the mind.

4. Move

Movement improves blood flow and clears thinking.

5. Melt

Grounding is an excellent way to stop mental chit-chat. It gives the mind a break and brings us back to physical reality.

- Breathe, nose, low and slow.
- Feel your feet on the ground.
- Be in the moment.
- Then continue with what you were doing.

Summary

To deal with stress, we first need to understand it.

- The first step involves understanding the nervous system.

EVENT ⟶ RESPONSE

Amygdala (the fear centre of the brain)

The key to creating emotional health

Widen the gap — stop, pause, feel, breathe

Learn the ability to self-regulate

PAUSE, BREATHE, RESPONSE, RESET
Event ⟶ Response

Frontal cortex (rational processing centre)

- The second step is to understand your language of stress and to learn to unpack it.

    – Stress is external and internal, positive and negative.

    – Anxiety is worry about a future event.

    – Panic is a feeling of fear, a sensation.

- The third step is to understand where you physically feel the stress, anxiety and panic.

There are three steps to helping treat stress:

- Step 1: Feel and express what your body is telling you.
- Step 2: Identify your triggers.
- Step 3. Implement stress-busting strategies.

CHAPTER 7

WHY DOES OUR BREATHING CHANGE?

From birth, we are hard-wired to breathe in and out through the nose, with the belly rising and falling as we breathe. This fundamental motor pattern is ingrained in us so much that babies can only breathe nasally and into their bellies for the first few months of life. That is unless their nasal passage is obstructed in some way or they have a medical disorder. It is not until they are around three or four months old that a baby will develop the reflex to breathe through their mouth. At about nine or ten months old babies start to experience emotions, and, at this time, they may start to use their mouth more as a default breathing system. From here on, the innate breathing pattern has the ability to change.

Common triggers of breathing change

Physical triggers

Mouth breathing

Mouth breathing and/or upper-chest breathing at rest is a waste of energy and it can change the body's homeostasis. We're not designed to breathe through our mouths. It's something that should only be used in an emergency or during high-end exercise. For many people, mouth breathing is only a habit, and takes no time to recorrect.

The nose is the first step, and if you cannot nasally breathe, it's vital to figure out why you may be mouth breathing. Is it due to a habit or an obstruction or an allergy?

If you do not nasally breathe regularly, the nasal lining can become soggy and boggy and inflamed due to reduced movement of mucus, which will create stuffiness and further prevent you from breathing nasally. Hence the term 'use it or lose it'—this definitely applies to the nose.

Nasal obstruction may result from something as simple as your glasses sitting too tightly on the bridge of your nose, thereby reducing the nasal airflow, or it can be caused by a common cold.

Thirty-five-year-old Sean presented with many of the symptoms associated with breathing dysfunction. He thinks he became a mouth breather following a bad cold several years earlier, and he says it's particularly bad at night.

The key change for him was reducing the stuffiness of the nasal lining with regular nasal rinsing (see section entitled "What drives a panic episode?"), relearning how to use his nose and altering the habit of mouth breathing.

Six weeks later, he was like a new man. He was waking feeling refreshed and he felt sharper mentally during the day. Most significantly, he realised his habit of throat clearing and coughing had gone.

In recent times, mask wearing has seen an increase in mouth breathing, and it is not uncommon to hear people say things like 'I feel like I'm suffocating', 'I feel short of breath' and 'I can't breathe properly' while they're wearing face masks. It is important to note mask wearing will not affect changes in our oxygen and carbon dioxide levels, but the discomfort caused can change the way we breathe as we may feel anxious.

Wearing glasses as well as a face mask can also result in mouth breathing. When we breathe out, it can cause our glasses to fog up, so we start mouth breathing, reducing the amount we breathe out to avoid this happening. This will affect our overall breathing pattern.

The increased work of breathing and the sensation of breathlessness both cause problems, which are more pronounced in people with underlying lung disorders. It helps if you ease into wearing your mask by practising for short periods of time while focusing on trying to keep your breathing regular, then try walking short then longer distances. It will take time to get used to mask use.

Posture

Try the typing test, then continue reading. This test reminds us that sustained poor posture can trigger altered breathing habits. This could be due to slouching at a desk all day or holding your belly in to achieve a flat stomach or simply breath-holding when you are focusing on a task.

There are even some job-related postures that can cause altered breathing. For military personnel, the guardsman's stance, belly sucked in, chest puffed up will be all too familiar. Soldiers fainting after having stood to attention immobile for hours is often caused by breath-holding. Ballerinas and gymnasts who have learnt the motor pattern of zipping up the abdomen so tight they can't breathe are also at risk of breathing dysfunction. For workers who require upper-arm movement, especially if it involves lifting their arms above their head frequently—for example, a postie reaching up to place mail in boxes—the double act of stabilising of the trunk and breathing at the same time can make their jobs more challenging.

Other mechanical causes may be as simple as splinting and protecting the belly after abdominal surgery, thereby forming a corset, which becomes a habitual puffer.

Obstructions

For those who have an obstruction—such as in children with enlarged tonsils or adenoids (please see chapter 10)—or the sports person as we saw in Toby's case history in chapter 4, who sustained nasal fractures. Surgery will be necessary before any effective breathing relearning can occur.

In the medical profession over the past decade, the area of orofacial structural development of breathing has grown into a big business. Specialties within the orthodontics field, and myofunctional therapy, have grown. Myofunctional therapy uses a combination of physical therapy exercises to improve the bite, breathing and facial posture of people with orofacial disorders. These practices predominantly focus on the development of the face and jaw and the resulting effect on nasal versus mouth breathing.

Sleep-disordered breathing within the respiratory field is another growth industry as it has recognised medically the importance of quality sleep. See John's case history in chapter 1 highlighting the effect snoring and his sleep dysregulation had on his health.

In 2019, the global sleep economy was valued at about US$432 billion. It is forecast to be worth US$585 billion by 2024.

TRY THIS TYPING TEST

• No matter how you are sitting right now, imagine you are typing an email, letter, document or sending a text from your phone.

• Now physically pretend to do the task, go, go, go, type, text, get the work message done, keep typing and texting and now stop.

• What happened with your breathing?

• Did you hold your breath?

> • What happened to the in-and-out breath, and the rate and depth of the breath?
>
> Remember that if you deviate away from nose, low and slow, your body will start to adjust and respond to the perceived new requirements or demands. If this happens regularly throughout the day, email apnoea can occur.

Email apnoea—life in the electronic age

This is worth noting due to the amount of time we spend using electronics. Email apnoea or screen apnoea occurs when people hold their breath while using mobile phones, reading emails or using laptops, computers and tablets. This causes muscles to become tight and tense. Breathing dysfunctions such as breath-holding, upper-chest breathing and reduction of abdominal belly breathing occur, resulting in an alteration in CO_2 levels over time, and through the course of a day oxygen levels can also reduce, resulting in an apnoeic episode (a temporary cessation of breathing).

Biochemical triggers

Allergies

Hay fever is the obvious one of these, as it causes a blocked nose, while asthma also has breathing pattern dysfunction associated with it. For some allergies, nasal spray and rinsing is the answer.

When I first met 16-year-old Katie, she looked pale, tired and lethargic. She had had seasonal hay fever since childhood. She had used nasal sprays intermittently but had never really done anything about it. Katie's nose was stuffy, and she was a mouth breather.

Her first step was to learn how important nose breathing is. Buy-in for this is essential, especially for teenagers. A healthy nasal hygiene regime was then implemented, including regular use of nasal sprays. It took time and regular reminders for her to breathe nose, low and slow but thankfully she persisted, and Katie is now a nose breather. She looks healthy and well, and when the hay fever kicks in Katie knows what to do.

Hormonal changes

Progesterone release, especially during ovulation and the premenstrual phase, can cause CO_2 to fall as much as 25 per cent. It's no wonder so many women experience pre-menstrual tension (PMT), headaches and irritability, and generally feel crappy.

The respiratory rates of women change throughout their hormone cycle. Progesterone is a respiratory stimulant, and it peaks in the post-ovulation phase. This can result in reduced CO_2 levels. These levels further decrease during pregnancy.

Speech

Speed of speech can trigger a breathing disorder. Rapid, breathless talkers maintain a poor breathing pattern while they are talking.

Work-related breathing disorders are commonly found in people who use their voice for work, such as untrained singers, call centre workers, teachers and lecturers.

Pre-existing conditions

Lung diseases such as asthma, bronchitis and emphysema can contribute to the development of breathing pattern disorders, as can postnasal drips, rhinitis, asthma, COPD, interstitial lung disease and metabolic disorders.

If a breathing pattern is improved, patients may experience improvements in quality of life and a reduction in some of the symptoms of their original condition.

Anaemia

Anaemia is worth mentioning as this is commonly seen in young females. Anaemia is a condition in which you lack enough healthy red blood cells (haemoglobin) to carry sufficient oxygen to the body's tissues. This will trigger a change in breathing and cause more rapid breaths as you try to increase the amount of oxygen to attach to the red blood cells. This is a medical disorder triggered by several factors and it must be corrected before breathing dysfunction is corrected.

Note: If you feel you are not breathing well and do not respond to suggestions in this book, see your GP as there may be an underlying condition driving the dysregulation. This will need to be stabilised before working on your breathing pattern.

Physical temperature changes

When we have a fever or a viral infection, we over-breathe in order to maintain internal balance.

Drugs—caffeine, alcohol, nicotine, aspirin, amphetamine, cocaine, crack, ecstasy, MDMA

Excessive use of recreational drugs, including caffeine and alcohol, can affect breathing. The stimulant substances are the main triggers. These are known as panicogens, which are chemicals known to cause panic attacks and anxiety. Key panicogens found naturally in the body are CO_2 and lactic acid. Even in the absence of stress, a reduction in CO_2 can trigger a panic attack.

Alcohol reduces brain–blood glucose concentrations. Coupled with altered breathing patterns, it can trigger symptoms faster.

Party pills can disrupt natural body rhythms and the balance of the sympathetic and parasympathetic nervous systems—the red zone/green zone balance. Clinically, I have seen many adolescents present for nervous system dysregulation post taking party pills.

The Mayo Clinic suggests that up to 400 milligrams of caffeine per day appears to be safe—a small cup of brewed coffee contains approximately 110 milligrams of caffeine. Caffeine is a respiratory stimulant, and levels of over 500 milligrams can cause effects like those of amphetamines. Amphetamines are stimulant drugs, which speed up brain body messaging in the territory of 4–5 cups of caffeinated beverages a day. Note that caffeine is also found in tea and many energy drinks.

Jason presented with chaotic breathing patterns. He was wired, his sleep was crappy, and he was exhausted. I struggled to work out what was causing his symptoms, then just as he was leaving, I asked him how many coffees he drank a day. His reply: 'About twenty!'

Education was the key to treatment here, and we made a plan to help wean Jason off his caffeine habit and reduce his coffee intake to two cups per day.

Blood sugar

Altering blood sugar levels can play a significant role in breathing, especially if there is an existing dysfunction. The brain needs both oxygen from the air and glucose (fuel) to function properly. These are transported around the body by the red blood cells. Breathing faster or deeper won't increase oxygen levels because the red blood cells become fully saturated with oxygen and cannot carry any more.

Blood glucose levels, however, may fluctuate a great deal depending on the type of food eaten, the number of meals and the time of day. Whereas sugar is released and used quickly, protein and foods low on the glycaemic index (GI) help to keep blood glucose levels stable as they are released into the blood stream more slowly.

It's recommended that individuals who are acutely hyperventilating try to consume protein or low-GI foods every two to three hours. This helps to keep blood sugars stable and minimises the symptoms of acute/chronic episodes.

Long breaks between eating can lead to fluctuations in blood glucose levels. Brain function relies on oxygen and glucose, so if glucose drops and oxygen is reduced due to a breathing disorder, symptoms such as loss of clarity of thought and dizziness may occur.

Laughter and talking

Excessive laughter and talking fast and a lot can trigger signs and symptoms if an individual is CO_2 intolerant. Both of these can drive CO_2 levels down.

Psychological triggers

Stress, anxiety, fatigue, panic, depression, overwhelm and persistent pain

Stress, anxiety and fatigue can all exacerbate and be exacerbated by breathing pattern disorders. Similarly, boredom, depression, learnt responses, misattribution, pain, history of abuse and trauma can have a significant impact. The breathing link to these has been covered in previous chapters, while pain is covered in chapter 14.

External triggers

Heat and humidity

Spending time in a hot, humid room for prolonged periods is known to alter breathing. As a result, we might pant to help regulate our internal temperature. If a breathing disorder is present, time spent in a hot, stuffy room can trigger this panting, which further drops our blood CO_2 level.

Once on the anxiety roller coaster, misattribution occurs and the individual might then think the space is the problem, when in reality it is the breathing dysfunction on top of over-breathing in a humid situation.

Hyperventilation in hot, humid air has also been shown to cause bronchoconstriction (tightening of the airway) in patients who have asthma, and cough responses and throat irritation in patients with allergic rhinitis.

Altitude

Altitude can also cause imbalances, resulting in over-breathing. If an individual already has a breathing pattern disorder, they often experience more symptoms with changing altitude. A common example is hyperventilating when flying.

Clothing

We've all seen the images of Victorian-era women squeezed into corsets to attain a minute waist. This fashion statement prevented them breathing deep into their bellies, so they had to breathe rapidly into their upper chests. This lowered their arterial CO_2 levels, which was a fast track to anxiety, panic and overwhelm, plus a heaving bosom and dilated pupils. It was not uncommon for women to develop dizziness and faintness, which was known as having 'the vapours'. When the corset was loosened—often after fainting—normal breathing was restored.

Instead of being treated as a result of tight corsets, the vapours were attributed to 'feminine hysteria', which was once a medical diagnosis for women who displayed symptoms such as shortness of breath, fainting, nervousness, insomnia, fluid retention, heaviness in the abdomen, irritability and loss of appetite. The easy fix to this one is to never bring back the corset as a fashion garment and to be wary of any constrictive clothing, even tight belts.

Factors in breathing dysfunctions

No matter what the trigger, once the dysfunction or habit occurs, it takes on a life of its own. The body can respond to altered breathing as quickly as within 24 hours, and then this can become the new norm. For example, when we have a cold, we often experience a blocked nose. When this happens, we learn to tolerate mouth breathing. Then, when the cold is gone, the mouth breathing and a potential new habitual pattern might remain. This can become our new normal and a disordered breathing pattern is established.

Whether the cause is trivial or profound, the first step is to restore normal breathing function, with the goal being to break this vicious cycle.

It's important to understand what is producing the sometimes frightening, and often annoying, symptoms, as the trigger and symptoms can determine the path of treatment. For example, if the breathing dysfunction has been triggered by postural or mechanical issues associated with neck or shoulder pain, then the treatment protocol will include a focus on movement in many positions.

If sustained pressure and life in the red zone are the major triggers and fear and anxiety co-exist, loss of self-confidence might be among your symptoms. In these cases, the physiological factors such as CO_2 levels must be considered, and treatment can include some good cognitive behavioural strategies from qualified therapists.

Summary

- Young babies can only breathe nasally.
- The mouth is a back-up, emergency system.
- Triggers can be physical, psychological or biochemical.
- It's important to note that in all of these situations, it only takes 24 hours for an altered breathing pattern to become habitual.
- An individual may recover from a virus or move to a different environment, but the breathing pattern dysfunction remains.

CHAPTER 8

A RECIPE FOR BREATHING WELL

Breathing covers a spectrum of needs, and it is important to know the best way to breathe in order to meet our needs at any moment, and how best we can move through sleep, rest, activity, exercise, sport, play, work, stress, ill health and recovery.

Breathing well means many things, so for the purposes of this book I have decided to focus on a few categories.

The first is relaxed breathing. It is important when considering how we breathe to always aim to achieve relaxed breathing at rest. This will take us into the green zone and put us into a state of calm. This is the ultimate and if you cannot achieve this, nothing else really matters as this pattern will set the fundamentals for movement and situation-specific breathing patterns. Relaxed breathing is the go-to we all should be trying to achieve throughout the day and before we go to sleep at night.

The second is breathing with movement, which I call effective breathing. Effective breathing refers to ideal efficient patterns of breathing for when we are moving.

The third is stimulatory breathing. The respiratory system and lungs need to be exercised and expanded to remain healthy, so stimulatory breathing practices are ways we can rev up our system to prepare us for a challenge or any other demand that may be placed upon us.

Finally, the rehabilitative component of breathing retraining is the base of physiotherapy. This involves breathing re-education related to ill health or other conditions—for example, breathing well with asthma or COPD, or following COVID, fatigue, surgery or injury.

Breathing well at rest and for relaxation is nose, abdominal, effortless, rhythmical, with a longer exhale. This is breathing in its simplest form, but nasal matters should always come first. Bear in mind that it can take anything up to six weeks or even more to recondition the body to use your nose.

Top tips to improve nasal breathing

Releasing tension

When you did the body scan in section entitled "Deep versus big", you may have found you had a tight, tense jaw. This will prevent nasal breathing, so try this exercise in which the emphasis is on the tongue and ensuring that it is resting in the correct place.

- Say the letter 'n' as in 'action' or 'Boston'.
- This places the tongue on the roof of the mouth behind the upper teeth, with the teeth slightly apart. (Your teeth should only touch when you are eating.)
- Keep the lips together and jaw relaxed.

Nasal rinsing

Habitual mouth breathers usually manage to successfully restore nasal breathing with nasal saline/bicarbonate rinsing to reduce nasal irritations. (See section entitled "Clearance methods" for a solution recipe and rinsing procedure.)

Nasal reliever or preventer sprays

Some mouth breathers may require a short course of an over-the-counter nasal reliever or a preventer spray. Keep use of these to a minimum, as decongestants dry up the mucus and long-term use can be harmful. Three days maximum in a row is recommended by pharmacists.

This will help to get you started on comfortable nasal breathing. The effects of these sprays are rapid, but not long-lasting.

Nasal steroid sprays need to be used regularly and consistently for optimal effect. It can take a few days of use to experience longer-lasting relief from symptoms. These require a prescription from a GP.

Note: Dosages must be checked carefully with the pharmacist. Reliever sprays should not be used for more than three successive days in order to prevent rebound effects, which may worsen the situation.

Nasal strips

Nasal strips, such as Breathe Right strips, and devices like Intake breathing bands help open the nostrils. These can be very helpful in the early days of nasal breathing retraining, especially during sleep. They can also be beneficial during exercise.

Ear, nose and throat specialist

Patients who demonstrate partial or complete obstruction of the nasal passages should discuss the option of a nasal scan with their doctor. This will help to find the source of the obstruction (for example, polyps, anatomical abnormalities, trauma). If required, the patient can then be referred to an ear, nose and throat specialist for further assessment and treatment. Once the nasal obstruction has been surgically removed, breathing retraining can commence if necessary.

Taping the mouth

Mouth taping, in particular at night, is a last resort. I only suggest taping if there is *no* medical reason for the obstruction. To do this, I recommend first nasal rinsing, then practising some relaxed nasal breathing using the Cottle manoeuvre, then place one thin strip of paper tape, such as micropore tape, vertically across the middle of the lips. This ensures that the seal can be easily broken if needed. Plus micropore is non-allergenic to the mouth and lips. However, this really is a last resort as there are so many other things you can try before doing this.

THE COTTLE MANOEUVRE

This manoeuvre can be used as an exercise to assist when practising nose breathing.

• Place your fingers on either side of your nose by your nostrils and pull outwards gently.

- Make sure your tongue is sitting behind your top teeth.
- Now try to use your nose.
- Gently nod your head, wiggle your jaw and raise then drop your shoulders. This will release tension in the head, jaw and neck.

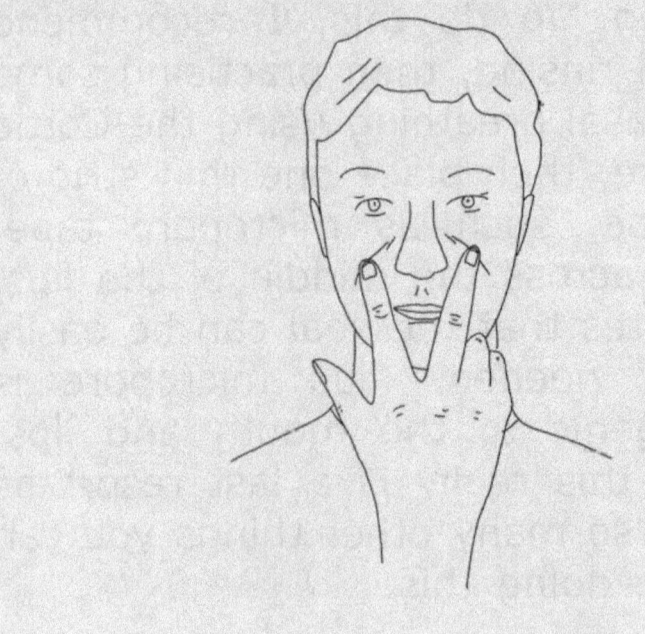

Other things that can help

1. Position
The beach pose is an excellent posture to try. In this posture, the accessory emergency breathing muscles are taken out of play. As they cannot

fire as easily, this enables the main breathing muscle, the diaphragm, to do the work of breathing, and it encourages an efficient abdominal breath. If lying on your back is not tolerated, try side lying or even lying on your belly.

Putting your arms above your head while sitting or putting your arms behind the back of a chair can achieve the same result. In standing, place the arms behind your back. All these postures help to turn off the accessory emergency breathing muscles. This is excellent in the work situation when you're trying to find the green zone.

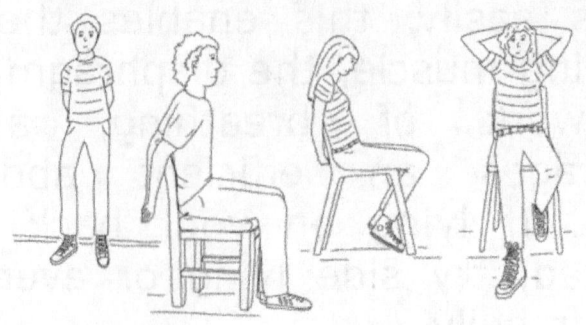

RELAXED, BASELINE, CALM BREATHING

Doing this daily takes us towards, if not into, the green zone.

• In a lying position, make yourself comfortable.

• Lie flat with a pillow under your knees.

• Place one hand on your chest, the other on your belly.

• Tune into your breathing—follow the breath.

• Are you nose and belly breathing? If yes, that is great.

• Just allow the breath to flow and enjoy it.

• Feel the gentle rise and fall of your belly.

• Feel and focus on the air coming in at the tip of the nose, and feel it come out the tip. This helps to relax the throat and vocal folds.

• Breathe in and out of your nose for four to six minutes.

• Expect the mind to get distracted as that is what minds do.

• Notice if it wanders off and, gently, kindly, bring it back to focus on the breath.

Mastery is attained when you can breathe in a nose, low, slow rhythmical pattern, with a longer breath out than in and with a slight pause at the end of the exhale, and this can be achieved without air hunger. Practise this for 5–10 minutes two times a day for six weeks to help establish a fundamental pattern and thereafter on a regular basis.

If you are not nose belly breathing:

1. Check your body tension. Remember if the body is tense, the breath will not flow effortlessly.

2. Is your nose clear? If not, follow the top tips to improve nasal breathing.

3. Is the abdomen moving first and most, and gently rising and falling when you breathe?

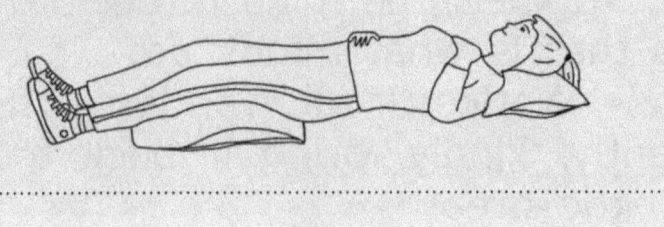

2. Feedback

When lying down, place a 1–2 kilogram weight—for example, a heat pack or a bag of rice—on your abdomen, then just follow the breath for a couple of minutes.

This will increase the awareness of where to allow the breath to flow to. The weight doesn't improve your strength, it just provides your body with feedback about where to breathe.

To reinforce upper-chest release, you can also switch the weight to just below your collarbone.

3. Reduce over-breathing/hyperinflation

If you need help to reduce over-breathing, try breathing out of your mouth through pursed lips. This allows for any trapped air to be released. Then rest the tongue behind your top teeth and try nose belly breathing again. Remember to breathe deep not big, as big drives us towards the red zone.

You could also try a gentle exhale through the mouth, a soft 'ha' to relax the throat muscles and vocal folds, and then breathe in and out through the nose into the abdomen. This assists in decreasing hyperinflation by changing the intrathoracic pressure.

4. Counting and ratios

Many breathing exercises include counting. I only use this as a last resort as it tends to break flow, but in some situations it can be helpful. It's a case of trying it out and finding out what your comfortable ratio is.

For a gentle abdominal belly breath, the preferred count is in for two seconds and out for three seconds then pause. This equates to approximately 10 breaths per minute.

Breathe in 1-2 and out 1-2-3 then pause, and in 1-2 and out 1-2-3 then pause and so on ... This is recorded as a 2:3:1 or inhale 2/exhale 3/pause 1.

The pause at the end of the out breath is important as it tells the body it's safe and it also prevents the CO_2 drop caused by over-breathing. Don't pause so long that you feel you need to gasp for the next breath though.

Try playing with different ratios to find what works for you. Eight breaths per minute equals breathing in 1-2-3 and out 1-2-3-4 then pausing, and in 1-2-3-and out 1-2-3-4.

When in doubt, breathe out

'When in doubt, breathe out' is the BradCliff clinic's motto. It is given to everyone who comes into our clinic. This is because when we breathe out, the heart relaxes, the muscles soften and we let go, and a message is sent to the brain that everything is OK. The longer the exhalation pause, the more relaxing the breath and the more relaxed we become.

Even though you might not think you're doing anything, air is still being exhaled. Most of us don't exhale for long enough. This is a common problem in particular with people who have conditions such as asthma.

SNIFF TEST

This will help to release any throat tension, while also reactivating the motor memory of nose belly breathing. It can also help to relax the vocal folds.

• Place one hand on your chest and one hand on your belly.

• Take a quick fast sniff in the nose. The sniff must be felt in the belly and must not be a nose chest sniff.

• If the sniff triggers chest movement first and most, this indicates a reverse breathing pattern. Work on this by trying to engage the belly sniff—breathe out through pursed lips, relax the belly, with a nice body posture, then try nose belly sniffing.

- Focus on the tip of the nose and belly button area, then do a quick fast sniff inwards as the belly moves outwards.

When practising, play with the pause, allowing it to be as long as you want. If you extend it for a long time, don't worry, you will find the breath in will gradually come again.

Take a breath in, then breathe out and pause gently at the end of the exhale. Now take a breath in and out with no pause. Do you notice a difference?

If you are not accustomed to relaxed breathing, you may find it difficult to pause. As you become more used to it, the pause will become easier and longer in duration. This will allow for relaxation of the shoulder and chest muscles and should decrease over-breathing and hyperinflation.

Breathing practice may feel strange initially, but, like anything new or different, it takes practice and time, just like learning to drive a car or ride a bike. Awareness of your breathing can be awkward initially and feel like a conscious action, but gradually awareness will become skilled and, with time, automatic.

If you feel or experience a sensation of not enough air—air hunger—swallow or breathe out through the mouth to release the tension and trapped air. This is your body making sense of the shift in the tempo of breathing at a neurochemical level. If this feels forced, stop and try again later. After practising this, always get up slowly, in case you feel light-headed.

When you manage to experience calm, especially if you have not felt calm for some time or you have had a breathing dysfunction for a long time, you may experience an emotional response—for example, laughter or crying. This is common and is known as a cathartic experience, an emotional release of tension.

It can take six to eight weeks to change an entrenched pattern, so be patient. It is suggested to practise breathing while lying down twice a day, initially for 5–10 minutes.

Checking in during the day is also essential. Habits quickly form, especially if breath-holding while concentrating during your day. This daytime pattern will set your pattern for sleep, so integrate checking in into your day using the BradCliff green dot method in chapter 6.

As an extension to the basic awareness of taking a breath, when you see the green dot, stop and do a quick body check for tension as well (see the tension check exercise).

Summary

- Breathing well at rest and for relaxation is nose, abdominal, effortless, rhythmical, with a longer exhale.
- The first step to breathing well is nasal health.
- Physical awareness and abdominal breathing come next.
- Initially, awareness will feel awkward.
- A cathartic experience, which is an emotional release of tension, may occur with baseline calm.

- Initially, it is recommended to practise twice a day for up to 10 minutes.
- It can take six to eight weeks to change an entrenched pattern.

TENSION CHECK

The order of tension release doesn't matter, so do these in whatever order works for you.

- Raise your shoulders and release.
- Pull your shoulder blades together at the back, then release them.
- Move your legs and pelvis.

Breathe out through your mouth if necessary (note, nose is normal) as we hold a lot of tension in the jaw.

- Breathe out as if you are blowing out a candle.
- Breathe in nose, low and slow. When breathing in through your nose and into your belly, aim for movement at belly button level.
- Breathe out, pause ... then continue what you were doing.
- And don't forget to smile.

Smiling releases pleasure hormones called endorphins, which are natural painkillers, as well as antidepressant hormones such as serotonin. A smile boosts your immune system, whereas a frown suppresses your immune system.

If you have to fake it until you make it, try putting a pen or pencil between your teeth as this mimics a smile, so even if you're not smiling your body thinks you are and will flood you with feel-good chemicals.

CHAPTER 9

EFFECTIVE BREATHING ON A DAY-TO-DAY BASIS

When we stand up, co-ordinated breathing and movement are essential for optimum energy efficiency, gas exchange and body homeostasis. When we move into the upright position, gravity influences us, placing more demand on our muscles and our bodily systems. This changes the breathing pattern as the muscles are required to work harder in order to pump more oxygenated blood into our bodies.

Effective day-to-day breathing still involves breathing into the abdomen initially, but the surrounding muscles will not be as relaxed as when we are sitting or lying down, so the belly doesn't bulge out as much while also acting in a more supportive role to the spine and abdominal contents. There is also movement felt at the lower ribcage, and the chest moves a little in rhythm with the abdomen. This is often described as bucket handle breathing. Imagine lifting a bucket by its handle. The whole handle moves but the top of the handle moves the most. In this case, the top of the handle resembles the diaphragm.

Body alignment becomes more important when we are upright. As more people live sedentary lifestyles, they adopt postures that can drive habitual inefficient breathing patterns. The most common poor postures are those adopted when using electronics. We call this 'chook head', but it has several other names including computer neck and forward head posture neck.

As can be seen in the image, the head is forward, the jaw is often clenched, the upper chest is tight and caved in and the shoulders are stooped. This is a disaster in the making. The first step towards avoiding it is to feel and identify reasonable alignment.

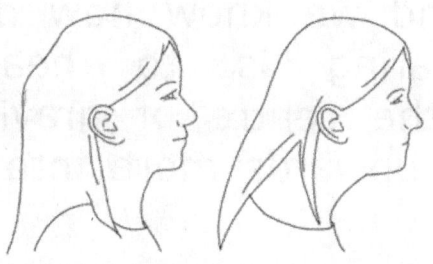

Poor posture

The two most common poor sustained postures are:

1. Slouched, where the body tends to cave in

There is no resistance provided in the abdominal cavity, so when we breathe there is little resistance for the diaphragm, and this causes inefficiencies to occur. The centre of gravity is displaced, usually into the upper chest.

2. Rigid, restricted posture

Movement is little and there is a lot of physical tension held in the muscles. This is common in breath-holding postures and the 'fab ab' culture. A tense back and abdomen works like a corset, and we know how detrimental corset-wearing is to health. With tension, the centre of gravity is also displaced upwards more into the chest region.

TRY THIS STANDING BREATHING POSTURE EXERCISE

- Stand with your feet shoulder-width apart.
- Imagine someone is pulling you up from the top of your head.
- Your ears should be in line with your shoulders and your hips.
- Gently breathe out, relaxing around your spine.
- Ensure you keep your ears in line with your shoulders and pelvis.
- Feel your weight in your feet, just in front of the ankles. Too far back or forwards alters the standing posture and creates pressure.

Relieving tension in the legs

Tense legs and pelvis are common when standing, causing inefficient diaphragm movement. Even if you are calm mentally, there is no way you will be able to breathe well when carrying too much body tension.

- Still standing, place one hand on your chest and one on your belly.
- Feel your breathing.
- Now focus on your legs, tighten them, and feel your breathing.
- Do a quick postural standing scan.
- Your feet should be shoulder-width apart with the weight just in front of the ankles. Loosen your kneecaps and wiggle your legs.
- Open your trunk so that your ear is in line with your shoulder.
- Gently chin tuck and loosen your jaw.
- Your tongue should be resting behind your top teeth.
- Now breathe out, breathe in, nose, low and slow.
- Aim for the breath to still be abdominal, but it may swing higher, just above the belly button.
- Keep your body in alignment, but soft and loose.
- What is the difference in breathing now?

• Did you notice that when tight and tense, breathing reflects this by moving more upper chest into the top hand?

Healthy posture

The advantage of breathing well and good posture is that less energy is required to breathe and move. There is also resistance for the diaphragm to work against and create the required pressure within the chest cavities.

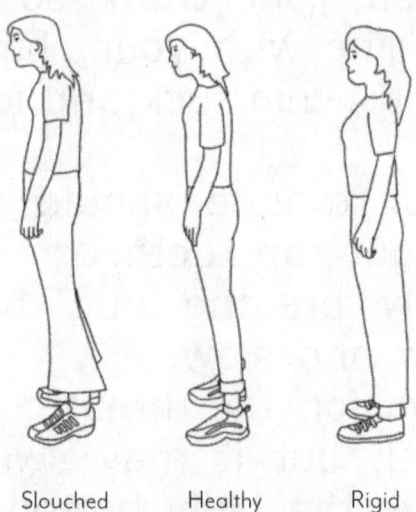

Slouched   Healthy   Rigid

TRY THIS SITTING BREATHING POSTURE EXERCISE

In a healthy posture, the earlobe should be in line with the shoulder and pelvis. This helps reduce chook head and a tight, tense jaw.

To find this position:

• Sit with your bottom against the back of the chair.

• Sit on your bottom (sit) bones. To feel your sit bones on the chair, move your bottom backwards and forwards until you find the middle point of pressure on these bones. This places the pelvis in a neutral position and it allows a healthy spinal curve.

• Open your trunk—increase the space from your belly button to your chest. This lifts the head up over the shoulders and loosens your shoulders.

• Lift your shoulders and release. Pull backwards and release.

• Now gently tuck in your chin back towards your neck and relax.

• Relax your jaw.

• Rest your tongue behind your top teeth.

Set yourself reminders to correct this position frequently throughout the day—at least once an hour. Eventually your muscle motor memory will click in, and this will become a habit within three to six weeks.

The key thing to remember is to move and to move often. If you want more information on this, *Breathe, Stretch and Move* is a great handbook full of stretches to help with posture and healthy breathing patterns.

Effective fuller breathing

Relaxed breathing only uses a small part of our lungs, so it helps to take a big full breath occasionally to ensure the lung remains healthy. This occurs naturally when we exercise at full exertion, or when the body takes a spontaneous sigh or yawn.

Occasionally take a big breath that expands the full lung. This means breathing using all regions of the ribcage, the upper chest, the middle chest and the lower abdomen.

To do a full complete breath, do the following:

- Place your hands on your abdomen/belly.

- Feel the relaxed breath.
- Then place your hands on the sides of your body and feel the breath.
- Then breathe into the lower ribs.
- Place your hands on your upper chest, and breathe the air into the upper chest.
- Work to allow a full, continuous breath.
- For a full exhalation after you have breathed out, gently tighten and draw in the stomach, forcing the remaining air out. Do this occasionally. This is not part of a regular practice or relaxed breathing, it is just a good, full, cleansing breath, stretching the lungs.

There is a natural movement pattern to the way we breathe, and I often use this known rhythm to help rehabilitate people. For example, following a stint in an intensive care unit, people are often physically deconditioned. If we can tap into their natural breathing pattern, it can help preserve energy and retrigger correct movement patterns. For example, breathing in when leaning forwards.

TRY THIS SITTING BREATHING POSTURE EXERCISE

In sitting, place your hand behind the small of your back.

Now take a slightly bigger breath in than normal, into your abdomen.

Can you feel movement at the small of your back?

If this is not happening, make sure your legs are relaxed.

Try again.

Does your back arch or flatten on inhaling or exhaling?

Match your breathing pattern to your activity

Depending on what you are doing, it is important to match the breathing patterns to the activity or task. As activity speeds up or demand is increased, our breathing pattern changes. If you move in a relaxed, graceful manner, you begin to feel this way.

Watch people walking down the street. If you were selling something, I am sure you would not hesitate to approach those who walk in a relaxed manner versus those who walk with a sharp, tense stride. This often reflects how they feel.

There are certain ways the body moves naturally in rhythm with our breath.

How you breathe as a rule

• When you breathe in, your back arches and your arms come up and out, and when you breathe out, the reverse happens.
• When you stand, you breathe in. When you sit, you breathe out.
• You breathe in when lifting your arms and breathe out when returning your arms.
• You breathe in when lifting and breathe out when lowering.

POSTURAL AWARENESS AND UPRIGHT BREATHING

- In sitting: Ensure your bottom is back in the chair. Your chest should be open and relaxed.
- In standing: Put your feet hip-width apart, pelvis in line, chest open, head up.
- Placing your hands on either side of your lower ribcage, breathe into your hands and the lower ribcage. This causes movement out and sideways.
- Put your fingers towards your stomach so you can feel this movement as well.
- Breathe to your thumbs at the back, getting movement of the ribcage backwards. This fuller breath occasionally is good to move air through the lungs.
- Breathing in through your nose, inhale steadily, allowing the abdomen to gently rise or expand. This breath should not be vertical.
- Breathe into the lower ribs, allowing the ribs to move sideways and backwards. Continue aiming for a rhythmical, effortless pattern.

- You breathe out when hitting, kicking, exerting during sport—the term 'exhale with effort' is a good reminder.

These rules are extremely helpful when working with someone who has poor respiration or capacity, such as chronic lung disease, or even post-viral fatigue, as it is all about movement and energy saving.

I often tell clients that when they're hanging clothes on the line, or reaching above their head, they should breathe in while pegging up washing or reaching upwards, and breathe out when dropping their arms back down. Breathe in when standing up, breathe out when sitting down. When lifting or hitting, breathe out. Exhale on effort, like a tennis player grunting as they hit the ball.

Breathing rhythms with movement add to co-ordination and energy conservation. In running and walking activities, we tend to co-ordinate our breathing and stride cycles. The striding to breathing ratio alters depending on the activity and level of fitness.

When walking, a breath cycle—which is a breath in and out—can occur over several strides. With low levels of activity such as walking, it is recommended that the exhalation stride ratio is greater than the inhalation stride ratio.

The key with exercise is to maintain rhythm and to co-ordinate breathing and movement. A sprinter has a faster rate, increased volume of air and no pause time. In walking, the rate is slower, less air is moved and the pause time is longer. Problems occur when there is a mismatch, such as breathing as if you are sprinting when you are walking.

The above breathing guidelines are taken from 'normal' values. Remember that our breathing is unique, and you're the best guide for your pattern.

WALKING

The rhythm of the feet provides a regular beat with which to co-ordinate your breathing.

• Walking at a normal pace, notice when you breathe in and when you breathe out. An inhale and exhale on heel strike is ideal.

• How many steps do you take to complete the breath in?

• How many steps do you take to complete the breath out?

• Try to take four steps to a breath in, then try five steps for a breath out.

• Change it up or change it down—try in for three, out for four, in for five and out for six.

CHANGING UP TO JOGGING

• Increase your pace and notice whether you are nose or mouth breathing.

• What is the step:breath ratio?

• Initially, start jogging breathing using your nose for as long as possible, as this increases your endurance—in through your nose and out through your nose.

• As the activity increases in difficulty, move on to breathing in through your nose and out through your mouth.

- As the pace gets harder, you can use your mouth to breathe in and out, but this is not sustainable.
- Try to ensure the breath is regulated and stepped. For example, breathe in one, two, three, and out one, two, three, or in one, two, and out one, two.
- Finally, on that steep hill, move to in one and out one—you may need to use your mouth.

Aim for a longer exhalation than inhalation, and rhythm where possible. The moment we breathe in more than we breathe out is when there is trouble. This can lead to a problem we call 'breath stacking'. This is when we breathe in more than we breathe out with each breath, which results in our lungs becoming hyperinflated and full of too much air. When this happens, you will become breathless quickly and fatigue easily as the physical limit of the ribcage and stretch of the lungs will trigger such sensations. Plus you quickly tip over the anaerobic threshold as lactate builds up in the muscles. This is prevented by focusing on the exhale.

If you feel you require assistance, see your GP to be referred to a skilled therapist.

Summary

- Breathing has an innate pattern with movement. Breathe in when reaching and opening the body, and breathe out when returning, bending, flexing.
- Breathing changes gears from standing to walking to jogging. The faster your pace becomes, the faster the rate of your breathing. It moves from your lower abdomen to your chest, and from the nose to the mouth.

CHAPTER 10

BREATHING WELL FOR ALL AGES AND STAGES

Babies and young children

For many people, there's nothing more enjoyable than watching a baby sleep. At night, we listen for the sound of our child's breath, while during the day, we observe their breathing patterns. Parents notice when their child uses their mouth instead of their nose to breathe, as this is often the first sign that they have a cold. Parents hear the gasps when their children cry, the gulping exhalations of laughter and their squeals of delight. As such, a parent is unknowingly observing their children's breath. A change in the sound of their breathing can alert us to our child being unwell. When the breath changes from a rhythmical, gentle pattern to a short, sharp, gasping pattern, we know something is wrong.

Breathing changes in response to emotion. From a young age, external factors and feedback from the external environment begin to mould who we are. Experiences in the world start to form memories, both pleasant and unpleasant, and we build a reference for responding to such stimuli. For example, when a child cries if they are hungry or need attention, and their caregiver responds to this cry, they learn that all is well and will settle quickly. However, if these cries go unheard or are responded to unfavourably, this reaction becomes etched in that area of the brain called the amygdala. When the amygdala is triggered too much and too often, it will take us to the red zone. Tempering the amygdala early in life and teaching your child how to self-soothe is vital. When I worked with survivors of torture and severe trauma, many of them had amygdala that were permanently switched on or 'running red hot'. The best we could do was to educate them on how best to turn it down, or how to temper it as much as possible.

By the age of five, children start to articulate how they feel and, as a result, should be much better at controlling their emotions. This is a key developmental phase of life, and breathing plays a role in learning the art of self-regulation, which is learning how to control your behaviour and emotions and to self-soothe.

For babies, suckling is vital for the development of the ears and the face. Healthy orofacial growth leads to the development of the palate and to open nasal passages, which together form the mechanical foundation for healthy breathing.

Signs and symptoms your child may have a breathing problem include noisy breathing, mouth breathing, persistent coughing or a cough that continues for weeks, excessive tiredness and irritability.

Dysfunctional breathing patterns can be caused by a variety of factors. For the young child, it can be from something as simple as nasal obstruction, through to more complex causes like trauma.

If a child is mouth breathing, you must find out what is causing this. It may be allergies or it could be merely a stuffy nose. Mouth breathing can lead to a variety of problems, including dental cavities, enlarged tonsils, or even a condition called obstructive sleep apnoea, which can really muck up sleep and focus and is even known to trigger ADHD. If mouth breathing is acted on early, a host of potential problems can be prevented.

Brain development is not complete until around 25 years of age, so this allows heaps of time for change, especially when it comes to self-regulatory strategies. When teaching a child or adolescent the tools of breathing well, they get it much more quickly and easily than adults do. This is because adults have often been entrenched in disordered habitual patterns for years.

Ten-year-old Sam is a lively child, but he presented with stomach aches, a disrupted sleep pattern and taking a long time to get to sleep. He had anxiety about getting to sleep to the point where his parents had to lie with him until he fell asleep. Sometimes, this wouldn't be until 10pm. He would then wake at 6am full of energy. As a result, his parents were tired. For the past six months, his behaviour had also become increasingly difficult, and Sam's schoolwork was starting to become affected. He had the odd stuffy nose and was a mouth breather. Sam also had a history of ear infections since he was a toddler.

The first step was to sort out Sam's stuffy nose using a saline nasal spray. Next, we focused on breathing well, and then added in the calm-down, bliss-out exercise (see section entitled "What drives a panic episode?") before bed. I also recommended the removal of all electronics and stimulants after 6pm. During the day, we asked Sam to focus on breathing out and using grounding as a way to calm himself down. Within two weeks, his sleep improved enormously, and

Sam now understands what calm feels like.

NASAL BREATHING EXERCISES FOR KIDS

Many of these exercises are the same as those recommended for adults. The key to getting children to do them is to make them fun. Here are some ways to encourage nasal breathing in both toddlers and children.

• Nasal rinsing is perfectly safe for children.

• Swimming in the sea can clean out the sinuses.

• Put your fingers on either side of their nose. Pull your fingers outwards to open up the nostrils (see the Cottle manoeuvre). Try to encourage your child to breathe through their nose.

• Humming (see section entitled "Increasing the production of nitric oxide") releases nitric oxide, opening the airways plus boosting the immune system.

- Drink through a straw while breathing through the nose.
- Breath-holding exercises can help (see chapter 11). The increased CO_2 also soothes nasal membrane tissue and reduces inflammation, so encourage your child to breathe in normally then hold their breath—ideally for 30–45 seconds on the inhale and 20–30 seconds on the exhale, if possible. They should only do this when you are with them, though.

BREATHING EXERCISES FOR KIDS

Teach your child 'when in doubt, breathe out'. When they really need to calm themselves and their breathing, try some of these exercises.

- Play the tissue game.
- Hold a piece of tissue paper in front of your nose.
- Blow out through your mouth with pursed lips while trying to keep the paper flying at a 45-degree angle (like this: \).

    – See how long you can keep the paper flying at a 45-degree angle without trying too hard.

    – The ideal goal is 10 seconds, but it's hard to achieve straight off. The majority of children I see start out being able to do it for four or five seconds, then gradually build up their time.

• Blow up balloons or blow bubbles.

• Lie a cup on its side on one side of the table, then take turns at blowing ping pong balls across the table into the cup, which serves as a goal, while timing each attempt.

• Using a straw, blow a ping pong ball across the floor or table, while encouraging breathing back in through the nose.

• Powerbreathe's flow-ball device (see section entitled "Airflow control") is an inexpensive and fun toy, which promotes healthy exhaling and encourages inhaling through the nose.

Also, try teaching your child how to do body scans and the relaxed breathing exercises in chapter 8.

These are ideal to use, especially just before they go to sleep.

Ear infections and blocked ears

Children who have recurring ear problems are often chronic mouth breathers. With the altered mouth-breathing pattern, the lymphatic flow is disturbed and becomes stagnant in the region of the head and neck. This results in fluid pooling in the middle ear, providing an ideal environment for opportunistic bacteria, which leads to infection. If your child is predisposed to ear infections, it is a good idea to check their breathing pattern.

Saline drops are helpful in loosening nasal congestion and clearing the upper airways. Talk to your chemist and try some of the tips above to encourage healthy breathing habits.

Breathing plays a role in learning the art of self-regulation, which is learning how to control your behaviour and emotions and to self-soothe.

New mothers

Sleep deprivation, hormonal readjustments and the demands on a new mother can make it feel like you're living in a war zone. Focusing regularly on nose breathing low and slow is a powerful weapon against anxiety and exhaustion.

When holding your baby or during breastfeeding, tune into your breathing, as one of the most important skills you can call on is relaxed breathing. When you breathe in a relaxed manner, it helps induce milk flow and production. The baby will feel your tranquil, rhythmical pattern as you breathe and this helps to calm and regulate their breathing in preparation for feeding.

The more relaxed you are, the better the flow and production of breast milk. This also sets the tempo for the baby's nervous system.

Adjusting to life with a new-born or toddler is demanding; don't feel guilty about taking small pit stops to release body tension and relax.

During feeding times

Check your posture. A straight, well-supported back with relaxed shoulders and a gentle, rhythmical, nose belly breathing pattern benefits baby and mother.

Beth is 32 and she has a six-month-old baby. She was tired, tense, sleep-deprived and just plain exhausted. Her breathing rate was high at 18 breaths a minute, while her pattern was chaotic. Her baby was not settling and had problems feeding. Beth had been screened medically and all was well with her physically.

After our meeting, Beth implemented regular breathing practices morning and night, and made an effort to really tune into her breathing just before and during breastfeeding. She supported herself on pillows, ensuring she was in a comfortable alignment. While holding her son, her arms were relaxed, her breathing regular and rhythmical. She was calm.

It only took a few days for her baby to respond to this new physical feedback. He too settled, calmed and began to feed well. Plus, he settled faster and slept for longer periods of time. According to Beth, life for them both seemed to form a natural rhythm. She felt this was due to her breathing well and feeling calm. She also noted that her voice sounded deeper and calmer, and she was aware she was speaking more slowly. She felt this new tone and speed of speech added to her son's ability to self-soothe in her presence.

Women's health

Pregnancy

Pregnant women often notice that they may experience shortness of breath. It can occur for two main reasons.

First, in pregnancy, the level of the hormone progesterone is raised. This decreases the CO_2 sensitivity in the respiratory centres and, as a result, CO_2

drops, causing an increase in ventilation, over-breathing or hyperventilation. Breathing rates may speed up by up to 50 per cent, causing havoc with the way we feel. Relaxed breathing assists in this phase and helps to counteract any hormone changes.

A GROUNDING EXERCISE

Children respond well to physical exercises like this. When they focus on their feet it is very hard for the rest of their body to be tense. I have found this exercise particularly good for children who have Asperger's and autism. Try the following:

- While either standing or sitting, focus on your feet.
- Starting with either foot, feel your big toe.
- Feel your second toe.
- Feel your third toe.
- Feel your fourth toe.
- Feel your little toe.
- Feel the sole and heel of your foot on the ground.
- Breathe out.

- Breathe back in the nose, low and slow and let go.
- Repeat this with your other foot.

Try doing this one with your kids as it is beneficial for everyone and it takes no time to integrate into a busy day, especially for an exhausted mum.

Second, the angle of the lower ribcage increases as pregnancy progresses. This displaces the ribcage outwards, which in turn compromises the efficiency of effective breathing. As a result, breathing can become upper chest and the diaphragm has to work harder. This causes an increase in the work of breathing.

It's important to work hard to ensure you are breathing abdominally at rest. This also helps the positioning of your baby in your pelvis, while calming your baby due to the low, slow, rhythmical pattern of your breathing.

Labour

Many women attending antenatal classes will quiz the teacher on how to breathe during labour, as if it is some special ritual to help in childbirth. The most important thing during the early stages between contractions is to breathe calmly and easily. This maintains a good blood flow to the uterus, which is beneficial for both mother and baby. It also releases relaxing hormones into the body, helping you stay relaxed, and helps to relax the pelvic muscles.

It is also common for women to hyperventilate during labour, so it's important to breathe out immediately after a contraction. The rule of thumb post contraction is to breathe out and breathe low and slow until the next contraction

Breathing during labour

Remember the different types of breathing between a sprinter and a jogger: one is for speed and the other is for endurance. Calm, easy breathing works to ensure endurance: think of it as a long-distance run, and so you must pace yourself to prevent fatigue setting in too early. You do not want to breathe like a sprinter and exhaust yourself too soon—this will only stress you and the baby.

As contractions increase

- Breathe in, breathe out, and let go.
- If contractions are strong, purse your lips (as if to whistle) and when you breathe out, blow.
- Try to get as much air out as possible, then breathe back in through your nose and repeat.
- Breathe out through pursed lips, letting as much air out as possible.
- The main focus should be to ensure all the air is expelled.
- Remember, 'when in doubt, breathe out'.

Note: With stronger contractions, the urge is to breathe in a deep, hyperventilatory manner. This can lead to problems associated with hyperventilation, often leaving you dizzy and short of breath.

In even stronger contractions, especially when you are not to push, focus on three to four blows out, pause, breathe back in via the nose in stepped fashion, so that the breath is not too deep, then blow out again through pursed lips. Blow ... blow ... blowww...

Infertility and recurrent miscarriages

Breathing well assists in both of these situations: the aim is to assist blood flow to the uterus. When you relax breathe, this increases the blood flow to the reproductive organs. Relaxed breathing also assists with total body relaxation, minimising stress and distress, and decreasing overall body tension. The pelvic breathing exercise is an excellent one to try for this (see section entitled "PELVIC BREATHING EXERCISE").

Menstruation and PMT

There is growing evidence of the relationship between respiration and hormones.

Progesterone is well known to act as a respiratory stimulant. Progesterone levels within the body are raised during the luteal phase (the phase prior to a period). For bad breathers, this increases the drive to breathe, leading to a further reduction in CO_2 levels of up to 25 per cent. Many patients tell me that when they have learnt to breathe correctly, they notice a reduction in their PMT symptoms.

Menopause

During perimenopause and menopause itself, fluctuating hormone levels cause varying degrees of symptoms. These range from minor aches and tiredness to hot flushes, mood swings and night sweats. The use of hormone replacement therapy (HRT) has been of great benefit to those with extreme and debilitating symptoms. However, various studies have indicated the dangers in prolonged or widespread use of these therapies.

For this reason, for women who cannot (or will not) take HRT, breathing education and relaxation and exercise programmes have been shown to be of great benefit. Like all self-administered regimens, these require the patient's time and commitment in order to reap the benefits.

RELAXED BREATHING

While sitting, place one hand on your chest and the other on your abdomen.

Focus on your breathing.

Feel your breathing, feel the pattern, feel the movement.

Feel it and think about it for a few minutes.

Breathe all the air out of your nose or mouth, and relax.

While breathing in, think about letting your stomach rise and let the air come into your lower hand.

Feel your stomach and your lower hand drop as you breathe out.

Try a gentle pause at the end of the out breath.

If this is difficult, try breathing in a little lower to the bottom of your lungs. The next breath will draw air into the bottom of your lungs.

Continue to try this pattern while aiming for a smooth, regular, rhythmical pattern.

Remember: nose, low and slow.

Focus on the breath out.

Gynaecological examinations and smear tests

These tests are not that pleasant for any of us. However, they are necessary for the prevention of ill health. The aim is to remain as relaxed as possible during these examinations as this assists in relaxing the uterus, which will help the procedure to be as painless and as comfortable as possible.

Teenagers

Resilience for teens

'My heart is pounding', 'My hands are slippery', 'I have pain in my chest', 'I feel dizzy'—feelings of panic, anxiety, low motivation and low mood are common in adolescents. Panic, anxiety and overwhelm are words that are being used by too many of our teens and sometimes even younger children.

While it can be scary to hear your child talking about these symptoms and using terms like panic and anxiety, it's important to listen to what they're saying and to try to unpack what's going on for them. It's possible your teen's sensations are related to their breathing. When we are breathing well, it's impossible to experience these sensations as intensely. As health professionals, we know anxiety is a felt sensation and that the first step towards resolving it is a breathing check-up.

How does your teen breathe? Nose or mouth? Upper chest or belly?

Very simple observations may give you a few answers as to your teen's well-being. Nose and abdominal breathing at rest is optimal—but the minute we start to alter our pattern at rest by mouth breathing or chest movement, we over-breathe and the CO_2 in our blood can lower within minutes. This can trigger a panic attack or the sensation of nervousness and anxiety, all of which are huge in this age group.

A range of factors trigger and sustain teens in a perpetual stress cycle. These could include a combination of mouth/upper chest breathing, over-breathing at rest, lack of food causing a drop in blood sugar, tight clothes, talking a lot and fast, excessive laughter, stuffy rooms and humidity. Each of these factors can change the way we breathe and—if a breathing pattern disorder is present—they can also trigger panic. Consider whether your teen's sensations may be related to this, and not to the misattributed causes they believe them to be.

Lucia is a pretty typical 16-year-old. She eats little or no food before a big night out, wears tight clothes and holds her abdominal muscles in to resemble fab abs. Her hormones are raging, and a stuffy nose causes her to mouth breathe. WHAM! This quintet tips the scales and her night is wrecked by a panic attack.

The first thing I did was to educate Lucia on the CO_2 cocktail that can spiral us towards a panic attack. She was relieved as she really thought there was something seriously wrong with her. The next thing was to teach her the five by five recovery breathing method, to *use when these sensations of panic occurred, to relax her breathing. The BradCliff apical deactivation technique was another excellent technique to help calm Lucia when she started feeling anxious (see section entitled "The older years"). This works well for teenagers as they can do it anywhere, especially crossing their arms. Lucia progressed well and was soon able to manage the sensations. To date, she has not had another panic attack.*

As CO_2 is a known panicogen, a substance that causes anxiety, if it drops too low or gets too high, we feel sensations of panic and anxiety. Some of us also have trigger-happy CO_2 tolerance levels, making us more sensitive to changes in our CO_2 levels than others might be. As a result of this, anxiety and panic are more easily triggered. The good news is breathing well and/or breathing rehabilitation from a qualified practitioner can help. The breath-holding exercise in section entitled "Breath-hold breathing" is an introduction to building up CO_2 resilience.

These sensations act as a strong reminder to stop and listen to our bodies

Encourage your teen to unpack what they are feeling and teach them about the CO_2 triggers.

The key is to not let these symptoms escalate. They are real and, if addressed early and *not* ignored, chronic conditions may be prevented and medication avoided.

The first step is to gently encourage your teen to consider how they are breathing. Get them to check their breathing pattern (see box entitled "TRY THIS SELF-CHECK"), and then use the corrective strategies in chapter 8.

The ability to self-regulate and self-soothe are two of the most essential functions we learn as human beings. Breathing well is the key to establishing these functions, and it is never too late to learn them.

PELVIC BREATHING EXERCISE

Lying down, first try what is called a pelvic tilt.

Lying on your back with your knees bent, gently rock your pelvis forwards feeling your spine arch off the floor as you breathe in while letting your legs relax a little and move with the rhythm. Now let go, allow the pelvis to relax back and repeat—aim for the action to become a rhythmical rock.

This time as you tilt your pelvis, breathe in. As you breathe out tilt your pelvis back to the floor. This breathing and movement co-ordination loosens up the pelvis, hips and legs, helping release muscle tension and improve the blood flow to the pelvis.

Pelvic neutral is found when the pelvis comes to rest in the middle of the upward and downward rock.

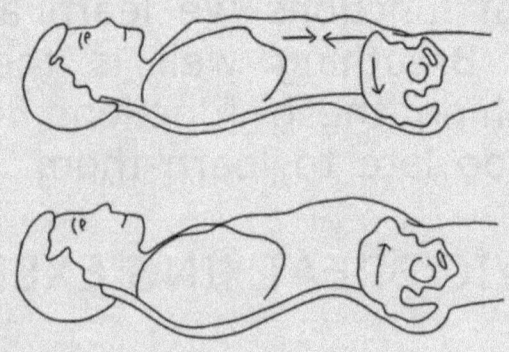

Over-training in sport

Having started my tertiary education in physical education, I am passionate about sport. However, in recent years I have seen the huge increase in training that is expected from adolescents, not only in hours but also intensity. As a parent, you must be mindful of this and be aware of the potential for physical and mental exhaustion in your child. (For more on sports performance including REP-5-energy deficiency in sport, and recovery, see chapter 11.)

Hypermobile, taller teens.

It is worth mentioning hypermobility, as this affects many children, and in particular our lanky, tall teenagers. We know our populations are getting taller each year. This increase in height creates a higher centre of gravity and, along with hormonal changes, make it difficult for teens to know where they are in space. This can add to hypervigilance, and hyperventilation which will further activate the red zone, the sympathetic nervous system, which in turn adds to the breath changes. Note if your teen appears to be hypermobile, as this is worth checking with your therapist.

Vaping

Navigating the emotions of adolescent life can be overwhelming, and many teens turn to self-destructive self-soothing behaviours such as alcohol, drugs, gambling, sex, shopping and vaping as ways to escape their emotions and feelings when things become too much.

Vaping is one habit kids are picking up in their droves, which is concerning as breathing is key for self-soothing. Data from a national survey published in the *New England Journal of Medicine* in 2020 showed that adolescent vaping in the United States more than doubled from 2017 to 2019. More than 25 per cent of US high-school seniors, typically 17–18 years old, reported having vaped at least once in the previous 30 days. This appears to be reflected in many countries around the world.

The main concern with vaping is the nicotine addiction that comes with it. Nicotine stimulates the release of adrenaline and increases the levels of dopamine, the reward pleasure chemical, in the body. In adolescents, this can affect the development of the reward centre in the brain and is far more likely to lead to nicotine addiction than in first-time adult users.

Once established, nicotine addiction is very difficult to overcome. Plus, it has been shown to lead to the use of stronger and more powerful drugs. Nicotine also affects the neurologic pathways that control attention and learning. To date, the medical profession thinks it may be safer than cigarette smoking but it is too early to tell. We still don't know the full impact of vaping on the lungs, but the flavoured juices cannot be good, as the lungs were not designed to be puffing in such large volumes of chemically flavoured steam.

The older years

Our lungs mature when we're about 20 to 25 years old, then after the age of 35 our lung and muscle function starts to decline gradually. By the time we reach our later years, we become more susceptible to lung-related diseases and disorders. The weakening of muscles and the diaphragm means we fatigue faster and experience more breathlessness. Often, this combined with a loss of healthy balance, known as proprioception, can cause us to lose confidence, which can lead to a reduction in the amount we move and exercise. This reduction in exercise occurs at a time when we should be embracing movement, balance and agility for as long as we can.

TRY THE BRADCLIFF APICAL DEACTIVATING TECHNIQUE

This assists relaxation of the upper chest wall and gently guides the ribcage down, placing the diaphragm at a mechanical advantage to begin abdominal breathing.

Place both hands on your sternum (breast bone), apply pressure downwards and hold gently, then focus on breathing out initially through pursed lips and breathing back in through your nose. Then try breathing in and out through the nose.

An alternative to this is crossing your arms and placing your hands under your armpits and applying pressure downwards, which achieves the same result.

This technique is excellent for those of you who find it difficult to nose breathe. If it is still difficult, try breathing in through your nose and out using pursed-lipped breathing, until air hunger subsides and you feel comfortable progressing to in and out through your nose.

It is also an excellent technique if you feel anxious or stressed, as it will help to trigger abdominal relaxed breathing and takes out the accessory, emergency breathing muscles.

Embracing movement needs to be encouraged and fostered. *Don't stop moving* even if it is just to walk to the letterbox or to get out of your chair and walk around the room every 30 minutes.

The key to healthy movement is balance, so try incorporating the balance exercise seen below into your daily routine. This is especially important as loss of balance in the later years is the biggest predictor of trips, slips and falls.

I do my balance exercises every morning while I am cleaning my teeth. I will stand on one foot at a time for about 30 to 60 seconds. This strengthens and keeps my balance system sharp.

Muscle strength

The loss of respiratory muscle strength can impair effective coughing and trigger breathlessness, both of which can have an effect on lung health. See chapter 13 for effective lung clearance methods.

Tops tips for keeping your lungs healthy

- Stop smoking.
- Follow the breathing exercises in chapter 8.
- Move more frequently, as this helps your lungs function properly. If this

is difficult, try the paced breathing exercises in section entitled "Paced breathing exercises".

- If you have a productive cough and lots of phlegm, please see chapter 13 for advice on chest clearance.

Raewyn is 71 years old. She's still fit and active and she works hard. She has completed most of New Zealand's Great Walks, and she preaches the motto 'use it or lose it'. One of her recent adventures was an e-bike trip around New Zealand's South Island, where she biked some of the incredible mountain trails in the foothills of the Southern Alps. This meant traversing some challenging terrain. Halfway through a steep incline on a narrow path, Raewyn was finding depth perception difficult. This resulted in her freezing with fear. She began hyperventilating and felt helpless as she knew she had to keep going.

The guide she was travelling with whispered a few words to Raewyn which made all the difference. He said, 'Just breathe, then get back on the bike and breathe.' So, she did. Raewyn completed the trail and realised she had a new mantra to help her when she's next confronted with adversity: 'Just breathe.'

The ability to self-regulate and self-soothe are two of the most essential functions we learn as human beings. Breathing well is the key to establishing these functions, and it is never too late to learn them.

Summary

- A child's breath is one of the first things that can alert us when something is wrong.
- As we develop, our bodies and minds adapt and alter. This blueprint of life can also alter our innate breathing patterns.
- Emotion changes the way we breathe.
- The hard-wiring of the system determines how we react later in life, but this can be changed and

tempered. Breathing well is the first step.

- If the mother is calm, chances are the baby will be calm.
- For teens, it is important to understand the language and feeling of stress, and to have the tools to teach them to breathe well.
- For older people, it is healthy to have a 'use it or lose it' attitude to movement and balance and lung health.

HOW STABLE ARE YOU?

Balance enables us to move on uneven surfaces, to glide when we run, to move effortlessly. However, it deteriorates with age and loss of physical awareness. With a few simple exercises, it is easy to maintain this integral skill.

TRY THIS

Stand on one leg.

Keep your hip bones level and do not let your hip drop.

Your non-standing leg should be bent 45 degrees at the hip and 90 degrees at the knee, so your foot is held behind your standing leg.

Your non-standing leg should not touch your standing leg.

Time yourself.

Approximate normal scores

AGE	TIME
20–49 years	25–29 seconds
50–59 years	21 seconds
60–69 years	10 seconds
70+ years	4 seconds

You can do this anywhere—standing at the photocopier, cleaning your teeth, talking on the phone, in the supermarket queue. Just stand on one leg for as long as you can without wobbling.

CHAPTER 11

SPORTS PERFORMANCE AND RECOVERY

Until recently, little attention has been paid to the breathing pattern of athletes. However, breathing is becoming recognised as a crucial component of athletic performance. For example, when runners wish to increase speed, they will take large, explosive breaths in synchronisation with their stride. In such cases, the breath increases proportionally with the energy output. If an athlete wants to sustain endurance, such as in marathon running, they will maintain rhythm and consistency of breath throughout the event.

In order to increase performance, the breath must be rhythmical, even in volume, and tailored to the task required. If an athlete has an inefficient breathing pattern when participating in their activity or sport, it can cause premature breathlessness or lower-limb fatigue, which is not reflective of their cardiovascular fitness. Alternatively, if they have a breathing pattern disorder at rest, this can impair their on-field performance, lead to anxiety and reduce recovery.

What Happens To Our Breathing During Exercise?

- As we start to exercise, breathing becomes deeper and faster, increasing up to 50 breaths a minute.
- Greater amounts of oxygen are required to reach the muscles and tissues. Larger volumes of air are moved. With exercise, the demand on the lungs increases 20-fold compared to that of the heart, which only increases 6-fold.
- Our relaxed pause phase is lost.
- We see the upper chest and often mouth breathing patterns emerge. Different muscle groups are called upon to work. The neck and shoulder muscles are called upon

to help with breathing in, and the trunk and abdominal muscles are called upon to help when we breathe out.

This is totally normal.

The stronger the respiratory muscles the less oxygen they require so they will literally steal less from other muscles in the body.

If they are weak this leads to a cycle as follows.

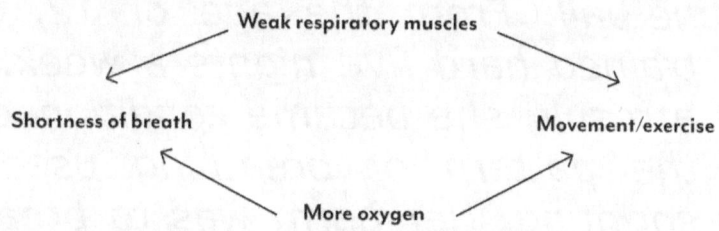

Rule number 1

Good strong inspiratory muscles, in particular the diaphragm, will help oxygen efficiency and energy levels. (See Inspiratory muscle training (IMT).)

Shortness of breath is not always harmful but can be merely indicating that the bodily demand is higher than the oxygen supply—it is your body's call to ease back, to allow it to recover and regenerate energy.

Rule number 2

Exercise must be balanced with bouts of rest, recovery and relaxation.

Jan is a retired sportswoman, who was a New Zealand secondary schools' representative runner in the 100 metres and the 400 metres, and who also played competitive netball. From the age of 12, she trained hard five nights a week. As a result, she became conditioned to the pattern of breathing used in sprinting. Her norm was to breathe large volumes of air into an over-expanded upper chest, then actively force the breath out.

The adrenaline this created was helpful for top-level competition. It gave her 'the edge', but no one stated the obvious—that she shouldn't breathe like that all the time. Her 'on switch' was triggered, and not only did she not know where her 'off switch' was, she didn't even know she had one. Her joints ached, and she often found herself hitting them to distract from the pain. Often, she also had sharp pains in her chest and between her ribs.

All of these symptoms disappeared when she was training or competing, which made her think she needed to do more rather than realising it was reinforcing her breathing dysfunction.

Her sleep was often disturbed, and it took her a long time to get to sleep. When her body showed her how tired it was, Jan would convince herself she just needed to get going again.

As a result of all of this, Jan's body began to break down and her injuries were slower to heal. Eventually, she felt she could no longer compete.

When I first met Jan, it was clear her breathing pattern was completely reversed, making her body more vulnerable to minor demands. Her breathing pattern at rest resembled that from when she was sprinting. As a consequence, *too much adrenaline continually flowed into her body. This created havoc and caused a host of signs and symptoms.*

It is not uncommon for top athletes to retire and develop bad breathing patterns. Many do not know what calm baseline breathing is, and this can result in an inability to truly rest, which is necessary for repair and relaxation. Luckily for Jan, she was able to restore baseline, calm, relaxed breathing patterns.

The importance of breathing well for sportspeople

In many high-performance sports, there has been a steady increase in the frequency of training and games. Along with this comes a demand for athletes to increase speed, strength and aerobic fitness—and, unsurprisingly, with that comes an increase in the frequency of injuries. All sportspeople go through difficult times, and it is hard to blame an increase in injuries on any one factor as there are always a number of contributing factors.

The pressure of selection, high levels of intense competition week after week, and overtraining, particularly in children and adolescents, have had a noticeable effect on both the physical and psychological health of sportspeople. This has become so common it even has a name—relative energy deficiency in sport, or RED-S. This condition occurs when people expend more energy than they gain from food, rest and sleep.

As athletes face all of these demands, it's important for them to maintain a healthy balance in all aspects of life. To do this, they need to ensure their recovery is optimal, and breathing well ensures quick recovery.

The increased pressure highlights the importance of not only physical agility but also mental agility. Breathing well can assist in both of these areas.

Breathing can be used to help with relaxation and focus, both during performance and in everyday life. Breathing well also helps to minimise energy expenditure when endurance is required. For example, if a player was to run several minutes while mouth breathing with their shoulders up around their necks, their energy stores would be used quickly. However, if their breathing is interspersed regularly with mouth–nose breathing and body tension is kept to a minimum, they will reserve more energy.

Different sports put different pressures on breathing and require different breathing patterns. Here are just a few of the more common ones.

Tennis

When I spoke to a professional tennis player about the importance of breathing, he said, 'When I walk back behind the court, I focus on my breathing. This allows for time, energy repletion and relaxation.'

You might notice how a lot of tennis players scream or grunt when they hit the ball. Not only is this noisy, but it has a function. The explosive breath out increases the energy released. In turn, this increases the force with which the ball can be delivered to an opponent.

Novice players will often breath-hold while they are learning, and they don't have the cadence of breathing and rhythm seen in elite players. It is not known whether these patterns are innate or entrained, so more research is required in this area.

Horse riding

Catherine is 34 years old. She is a competitive equestrian. She clearly understands the importance of breathing well in her performance. 'The most interesting thing I've learnt is when I breathe well, my horse is easy to control. When he is misbehaving and not responding, I realise that I've either been holding my breath or breathing so shallowly and rigidly that he has responded to my tension.'

Golf

When hitting the ball, breathing and movement and cadence are important. For example, breathe in while swinging up and back, then breathe out—one, two, three—as you swing forward.

When walking between holes, focus on grounding and take recovery breaths to help you retain focus and calm performance nerves. Golf coaches talk about breathing freely, as this increases your performance.

Running

Should you breathe through your nose or mouth when running? The answer is a big, fat 'It depends!'

If you are sprinting, you will need a large amount of air coming in at speed, so absolutely you will need to mouth breathe. However, while endurance running at a lower intensity, the nose will do a great job.

In the early 2000s, the 80/20 rule entered the world of endurance training thanks to research by exercise scientist Stephen Seiler. This rule states that an optimum of 80 per cent of training should be done at low intensity. This has led to an awareness of just how hard we tend to push ourselves at high intensities, which is stressful to the body.

The nose does a great job at keeping us in the aerobic, lower-intensity zone, so much so that some long-distance runners breathe nasally throughout their events. This gives them a continuous release of energy while preventing them from hitting the anaerobic threshold, which will push them towards fatigue and exhaustion. This is totally doable, but it takes practice and training.

Pip is 45 years old. Growing up, she had asthma, hay fever and was allergic to every furred and feathered creature her family owned. In her twenties, she took up running and soon realised her years of mouth breathing were becoming a problem. Breathing was her limiting factor as her chest felt tight and her neck and shoulders got sore.

Her first step towards changing her breathing patterns was to learn to breathe nasally when she was at rest. This involved sinus rinsing, learning to 'slow the flow' and to breathe gently rather than forcing the air in. Early in this process, she also used nasal strips to help keep her nostrils open. According to Pip, the air hunger took time to work through, but she eventually managed to form new breathing habits.

With her breathing patterns addressed, Pip had to learn to slow down to a pace her nose was happy with when she was running. This can be difficult for some people to deal with, as pressure from peers and coaches as well as the ego can interfere here. Taking time out to train alone during this time can be useful. The ability to flare the nostrils can also be an issue, as these muscles can get a bit lazy and need some encouragement or help. If this is the case, try using nasal strips or devices that crank the nostrils open.

Over time, Pip noticed her chest was no longer tight and she no longer needed her asthma inhaler. This can be attributed to a few factors:

1. *Ensuring that she warmed up at an easy pace. This causes the nose to warm, and as it does it filters and humidifies the air before it hits the lungs, thereby reducing the likelihood of airway sensitivity and bronchospasm associated with asthma.*

2. *Breathing nasally means we lose 42 per cent less water than when breathing through the mouth. When running, Pip no longer required as much hydration and was able to take on nutrition without choking while she was racing.*

3. *Her neck and shoulders felt relaxed as breathing through the nose recruits more lower-rib/diaphragm activity, which is sustainable for longer. Conversely, breathing through the mouth tends to recruit our neck/shoulder girdle muscles, which requires more effort.*

A few years after Pip did the work to change her breathing patterns, she took part in a treadmill test to measure her blood lactate levels. The results of this showed that her previous mouth breathing put her in a higher heart-rate zone than she needed to be in to build efficient aerobic endurance. She had been going out too fast and into anaerobic or higher heart-rate zones, which is stressful on the body and unsustainable for longer runs.

By altering her breathing so she can run at nose-breathing pace, Pip kept herself in lower heart-rate zones, which meant she could better pace herself for longer events. As a result, her running is far more efficient and her recovery quicker.

Scuba diving

When diving, breathing is used to fine-tune buoyancy. When diving, a buoyancy control device (BCD) is worn. This enables divers to drop to the depths or rise up as necessary.

For example, when swimming and to rise up over obstacles or go to the surface, a breath in will help create buoyancy and lift you up. Conversely, when breathing air out, the exhalation will help to lower you deeper into the water.

Breathing is also useful for relaxation when diving. Many novice divers chew through their air as they are nervous and unfamiliar with the process, which causes them to breathe rapidly. However, when they use a regulated and relaxed breathing pattern, they will use far less air, which in turns helps them to relax further.

It is not uncommon for patients who have an upper-chest, large-volume breathing pattern to find it hard to stay on the bottom of swimming pools, yet they have no problems at all floating.

Surfing

All surfers are aware of the importance of breathing well physically, as well as the ability to breath-hold, as surfing often involves time spent under water.

Swimming

Breathing control is very important when swimming. Your breathing must be co-ordinated with your body movement. As such, it is an excellent exercise to develop the lungs and co-ordinate breathing with movement. I often recommend my patients to take up swimming as an exercise, and tell them to focus on ensuring their breathing and arm-stroke cycles have an even pattern.

Boxing

Nasal breathing is essential for boxing, so the mouth stays shut protecting the teeth. The key thing is to breathe out when you throw the punch as this helps to release an immense amount of energy.

Martial arts

Martial arts combine the breath with physical and mental exercises, which is brilliant. In Chinese martial arts, they believe that if the untrained body were as erratic in its movements as the untrained mind, a person would be lucky to make it through a single day unscathed. They believe that a trained body is impossible without a trained mind, and they use the process of meditation to attain this.

Weight-lifting

When lifting weights, it is recommended that you breathe out as you lift the weight. With deadlifting, athletes often take a breath in then perform a Valsalva manoeuvre, during which they brace the belly and hold the breath, then as they lift the weight, some will exhale after they pass the tough point of the lift. All of the above are guidelines for awareness. Each of these techniques should be taught by a professional, as they are not as simple as they sound. Each sportsperson has their own unique movements and breathing patterns that require training. However, if you start with the basics suggested in this book, you will have some knowledge and awareness of where improvement might be made.

Oxygen and carbon dioxide for sportspeople

Ultimately, to achieve our goals and do what we want to do, we need energy and good health. These give us the tools to complete tasks and succeed. There is no success without healthy, oxygenated cells. Health of tissues, whether mind or body, is dependent on the delivery of oxygen. For sport, the more oxygen to muscles the better. Oxygen is delivered from the lungs into the blood stream. A deep belly breath helps as the lower lobes are the most oxygen-rich lobes in the body.

Once in the blood stream, delivery is breath-dependent, from the mechanics of the vital pump to the ability of CO_2 to open up the size of the blood vessels. Low CO_2 causes constriction of the blood vessels, so good, healthy breathing helps. For serious athletes, it also helps to learn to tolerate higher levels of carbon dioxide as this has several benefits.

Prolonged breath-holding helps oxygen conservation in the blood flow to vital organs, a reduction in heart rate and an increase in arterial blood pressure. The ability to breath-hold often increases with relaxation and efficient breathing patterns.

At rest and while sitting, occasionally practise a gentle breath-hold at the end of either the inhale or exhale, just to check your CO_2 tolerance. Just note that if you're unwell, it will be pretty poor.

James is a 24-year-old competitive triathlete. I first met him for a breathing tune-up three days before a big race. All of his markers were excellent except his breath-hold inhale was just seven seconds. I was so shocked by this that I repeated the test several times. When he left the clinic, neither of us was any the wiser about what was causing this.

The following day, James came down with a virus that prevented him from competing. My take-home from this was to test most people with the breath-hold, as this hidden gem of information is a great indicator of what is happening at a cellular level.

GROUNDING EXERCISE

This exercise is good for all stressful situations. You can do this while standing or sitting.

• Feel your feet on the ground beneath you.

• Feel your toes on the ground.

• Feel your big toes. Feel your second toes. Feel your third toes. Feel your fourth toes. Feel your little toes.

• Feel the balls of your feet.

• Feel your heels and your inner arches.

• Soften your knees and jiggle them a few times.

• Soften your shoulders and jaw.

• Breathe out while focusing on your feet (through the mouth if necessary).

• Breathe in through your nose and abdomen.

• Continue this exercise until you feel in control, focused and calm.

If you need a grounding exercise to use while on the field or during a speech, try the one below. It only takes a few seconds and can be done anywhere. These steps will help to calm the nervous system and reduce the amount of adrenaline pouring into your body. It's a quick exercise that will allow you to become present.

- When panic sets in, pause then exhale.
- Focus on the sensations in your body, in particular your feet, which are firmly planted on the ground.
- Look to the horizon, as this triggers the parasympathetic nervous system to kick in.
- Refocus.
- Stop your thinking mind and any intrusive thoughts.
- Adopt a recovery posture if necessary.

Performance anxiety

Prior to any event, no matter what it is, performance anxiety is not uncommon. This applies to anyone, whether you are competing at the Olympics, going for an interview, standing up in front of the class to read your homework, or speaking at a friend's wedding.

Common sensations include throat tightening, stomach clenching, hands becoming clammy, the voice quivering and breathing speeding up. At its worst, you may break into total panic as your thoughts become disturbed. Palpitations, dizziness, nausea and vomiting might even occur. You feel petrified of losing control. Breathing becomes more laboured, so anxiety increases—it acts as a feedback loop. The thinking mind kicks in, searching the memory library for past experiences. 'I am not good enough', 'I can't do this', 'I am going to embarrass myself' and so on.

Almost everyone is familiar with the above symptoms. While in the theatre, it is known as stage fright, in the business world, it can be perceived as incompetence.

It is well known that moderate levels of adrenaline enhance performance. The important factor is your ability to regulate these feelings, so that you are in control. Break the vicious cycle! Breathing is one of the most powerful tools you have when you're feeling anxious or overwhelmed.

The difference between relaxation and downtime

When I ask people what they do to relax, the most common answers are watch a show on Netflix, read a book, exercise and listen to music.

CARBON DIOXIDE TOLERANCE TEST

For the body to function optimally, CO_2 plays a critical role. As such, CO_2 intolerance can be a major inhibitor to health. To find out how you tolerate CO_2, try this breath-holding exercise.

- Use the stopwatch on your phone or find a timer.
- Sit in an upright position and relax.
- When you are ready, take a couple of normal, relaxed deep breaths in and out.
- At the end of the exhale (the out breath), hold the breath and

record your time. Do this for as long as you feel reasonably comfortable. You do not want to go red in the face. Note: At about 10 seconds, the breath reflex will kick in and you may feel a wee kick in the upper gut region.

• Breathe normally again, nose, low and slow for a few minutes.

• Repeat the breath-hold, but this time do it at the end of the inhale instead of the exhale.

The average time for these breath-holds is 30 seconds at the end of the exhale and 40 seconds at the end of the inhale. If your times are significantly shorter than this, it may indicate a physiological or mechanical imbalance.

I am not sure about you, but the series that I watch on Netflix are *not* relaxing. The same goes for exercise. As they're not relaxing activities, I call these *downtime* activities.

There is a massive difference between downtime and relaxation, and it's vital that you know and understand this distinction. This is essential for everyone, whether they're recovering from sport, surgery, illness or just the stresses of day-to-day life.

The dictionary definition of 'relaxation' is: 'the state of being free from tension and anxiety'. Therefore, relaxation is the flipside of performance.

True relaxation strengthens the immune system, and allows repair and regeneration via the release of powerful hormones, while also creating mental alertness and sensations of emotional calm and clarity.

Research shows that breathing strategies are critical for any relaxation techniques to be successful.

Three steps to relaxation

1. Physical awareness

Feel your body and learn to let go. To help with this, use the exercises in box entitled "TRY THIS SELF-CHECK", or do a quick body scan (see section entitled "A quick, relaxing body scan").

2. Understand the difference between the green zone and the red zone

True relaxation can only occur when you are 100 per cent in the green zone.

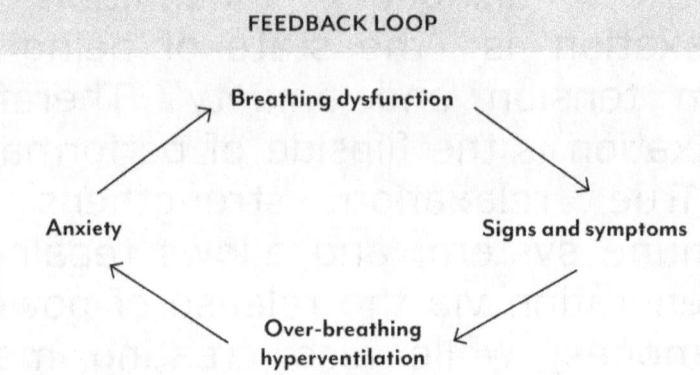

FEEDBACK LOOP

Breathing dysfunction

Anxiety

Signs and symptoms

Over-breathing hyperventilation

3. Practise

Practise in many situations and places. Use the green dot method and learn to make this part of your everyday practice. Just as we learn to clean our teeth, we should also learn to do a daily relaxation practice. Whether for just a few seconds or longer, this will ensure we last the distance. There are many methods for you to try. The BradCliff calm-down, bliss-out exercise is a quick and easy routine you can implement anywhere.

Recovery breathing

Sport-specific, energy-efficient breathing assists with all sports. Good breathing patterns at rest are essential. This ensures you are starting from a mechanical and physiological advantage.

Immediately after exercise, step down your breathing pattern. Initially, big mouth breaths will occur. Work to reduce the size of these breaths, then move from mouth to nose breathing. In the case of explosive exercise, unless this is done, hyperventilation may occur.

Jack and Ella are both teenage national-level athletes. They each struggle to get their breath and find form, and both have upper-chest breathing patterns, with resting respiratory rates well over 18 breaths per minute. No wonder they were both literally falling to bits by the time they reached the clinic! They had both seen numerous specialists, and had been diagnosed and treated for vocal cord dysfunction. Treatment for this made a small difference, but their symptoms continued. They were both told they were stressed out, so went to see a psychologist. This gave them no resolution of their symptoms. They were each struggling to find the psychological stressors to explain their symptoms, which they thought were fuelling this dysfunction.

Yes, they were stressed, but not in the way the specialists thought. Their breathing patterns were dysfunctional, keeping them both revved up and in the red zone.

Mechanical and physiological breathing dysfunction can be hidden behind 'stress'. The incredible stress these athletes were under was both mechanical and physiological. Their breathing was reversed—upper chest first and most—and their lungs dynamically hyperinflated.

Treatment was initially kept simple and involved reducing the work of breathing and calming the nervous system. This was followed by strengthening their breathing and motor patterns, then co-ordinating all of this with movement. The *strengthening included inspiratory muscle training.*

Both Jack and Ella responded very quickly, as teenagers do, and both presented at their follow-up sessions looking better and with much better breathing. They each reported feeling calmer and physically stronger.

Treatment involves these basic recommended strategies:

- Knowing what basic breathing at rest is. It was essential that they felt the deep calm associated with the green zone. See the BradCliff calm-down, bliss-out in box entitled "BRADCLIFF BREATHING CALM-DOWN, BLISS-OUT EXERCISE: FOR A QUIET BODY AND A QUIET MIND".
- Warming up prior to sport using the grounding strategies found in section entitled "EXERCISES AND OTHER STRATEGIES".
- Inspiratory muscle training (IMT).
- Breathing for rest and recovery, baseline calm, see box entitled "RELAXED, BASELINE, CALM BREATHING".

Breathlessness

Breathlessness disproportionate to fitness is common in sportspeople. This is another symptom of breathing dysfunction. Pursed-lipped breathing during sport can help reduce this sensation. It also helps to prevent the phenomenon called breath stacking (see chapter 9).

Breath stacking in sport occurs when a breath is not fully exhaled before another breath is taken in, so stacking one breath upon another until reaching a point where the lung is stretched and a sensation of breathlessness is triggered.

Breathlessness may also be the result of exercise-induced bronchospasm (EIB) or exercise-induced laryngeal obstruction (EILO).

Choking during sport

This is when an athlete fails to manage anxiety and cope with the demands at a crucial moment. This can lead to a catastrophic drop in performance. As it is vital to bring the athlete back to the present moment quickly, I recommend implementing grounding exercises and knowing the appropriate recovery postures.

Recovery postures

Adopting any one of these postures can help you to switch off the over-breathing muscles and trigger abdominal breathing, which will send you back towards the green zone. Recovery postures also aid recovery on the field or during performances (see section entitled "Recovery or rest positions").

Summary

- In high-performance situations, whether on the sports field or in the office, breathing patterns need to be finely tuned and situation-specific.
- To counter performance anxiety, perform a grounding exercise.

Exhale with effort

- Focus on steady rhythmical patterns—find your striding breathing ratio.
- Practise good basic abdominal breathing patterns in various optimal postures. This is to reinforce the correct motor control patterns of muscles.
- Prior to competing, use nose, slow, low breaths for calming the nerves.
- There's a difference between downtime and relaxation. Downtime is watching TV, reading a book/magazine or exercising. Relaxation is a conscious practice to still the body and thought processes.
- If you feel good, you think well.

CHAPTER 12

SPEECH—BREATH AND VOICE PRODUCTION

The expression of emotions through speech and sounds, and the corresponding ability to perceive such emotions, are both fundamental aspects of human communication. We all know the saying 'I just needed to get that off my chest.'

In order to speak, we need to have a voice. Breathing is the foundation of good voice production. The voice is produced by the breath striking the vocal folds (formerly known as cords). The throat, tongue, lips and soft palate modify sound, and the quality of the voice is affected by air escaping from the nose. An example of this is the way the sound we make alters when we have a blocked nose.

The control of airflow assists with good voice production. For this to occur, good abdominal breathing is important. Laughing, coughing, crying and the hiccups are void of this control as they are all reflex actions.

Coughing is an important defensive reflex against foreign bodies, while crying is a survival reflex. Think of babies—crying is their way of expressing that they require something. Scientists are uncertain what the hiccup reflex is associated with, but they think it is sometimes the result of the diaphragm becoming irritated. When this happens, it pulls down in a jerky way, which makes you suck air into your throat suddenly. When the air rushing in hits your voice box, your vocal folds close suddenly and you're left with a big hiccup.

Voice control

People with breathing pattern disorders often speak rapidly, their sentences punctuated by sighs, gasps and audible inhalations. The voice strength and tone fades with increasing pitch towards the end of a sentence as airflow is reduced.

Abdominal breathing is one of the most important tools you have in controlling voice. A disturbance of this pattern can lead to or contribute to a voice problem. According to a report, one worker in three in the world's modern economies relies on their voice, while up to a quarter of employees experience voice problems. These people seem to talk continuously in a steady stream only to gasp for breath before taking off again. Many of these people have a defective breathing pattern. Interestingly, research into the preferences of employers when looking to employ have shown that the ability to clearly communicate verbally has consistently been number one.

The first step for adequate speech is good abdominal breathing (see chapter 8). Talking fast with uninterrupted sentences riddled with sighs and gasps not only sounds bad but can also cause CO_2 levels to drop.

Symptoms of chronic hyperventilation—dizziness, detached sensations and even panic—can occur during or after talking if someone already has a breathing dysfunction and CO_2 instability.

It is not uncommon for people in talking professions to complain of symptoms. Common among these people are teachers, lawyers, actors, singers, call centre workers and salespeople. These people often report difficulties with breath control and vocal tone. Loss of confidence and performance anxiety are common as a result.

The mechanics of speaking and breathing

What is speech?

Speech is a complex motor task involving co-ordination and timing of muscles, air and movement, which involves vibration of the vocal folds, a good intra-abdominal pressure and diaphragm control. Good posture and breathing control are also essential.

HOW TO STOP HICCUPS

Hiccups can be stopped by increasing carbon dioxide, so the idea of breathing in and holding at the top of the in breath makes sense.
- Take a breath in.
- Hold it for 10 seconds.
- Then swallow.

Vocal problems

This is a common problem for habitual over-breathers. The following are some of the problems that lead to altered speech:

- Habitual mouth breathers with blocked noses or sinus problems commonly report sore or dry throats. They also sniff or clear their throats frequently, often to the annoyance of others. Note: Sinuses serve as resonating chambers for speech, so if these are stuffy, sound will be affected immediately.

- People suffering from anxiety or depressive disorders with increased sympathetic arousal and physical tension, and upper-chest or mouth breathing often have jaw and throat tension as well. They tend to speak in a monotone.

TRY THIS TO CHECK YOUR AIRFLOW

The airflow from breathing out assists with good voice production.

• Breathe in and as you do speak at the same time. It is extremely difficult.

• Now breathe out as far as you can by using your nose, mouth and lungs.

• Now try to speak. Yet again, this highlights how vital good, controlled airflow is for speech.

- Patients with a history of hiatus hernia, gastro-oesophageal reflux disease (GORD) or laryngopharyngeal reflux (LPR) frequently complain of irritated throats, chronic throat-clearing and huskiness.
- People with problems with vocal fold dysfunction (VCD), EILO or dysphonia.

Both coughing and throat-clearing are necessary actions because they clear the respiratory passageway, but they also place the vocal folds under significant strain. (See chapter 13 for cough and chest clearance techniques to help avoid habitual coughing or throat-clearing.)

Vocal fold disorders

Awareness of vocal fold disorders has increased over the past decade. Vocal fold dysfunction, also known as inducible laryngeal obstruction (ILO), is the inappropriate closure of the vocal folds when we breathe in. This causes shortness of breath and may occur during strenuous activity.

TRY THIS SPEAKING TEST

- Practise reading out loud from a book and record yourself.
- Then do a calm-down, bliss-out exercise.
- Follow this with humming until your lips tingle.
- Read the same passage out loud and record yourself again.
- What do you notice?

The symptoms of this disorder are often confused with asthma, so clients will often present saying they have a diagnosis of asthma. The tell-tale signs are:

- a high-pitched sound caused by a blockage in the throat or voice box, which is known as stridor
- difficulty when breathing in, while with asthma the difficulty is when breathing out
- throat tightening, whereas in asthma the chest tightens
- dysphonia (abnormal voice) during or following an attack
- episodes come on quickly and can resolve quickly
- little or no response to medical treatment, meaning inhalers, such as bronchodilators, don't make any difference.

The most common causes are thought to be exercise, irritants and stress.

When exercise-induced laryngeal obstruction (EILO) comes on, it can be a scary experience, as the individual will feel as if they suddenly cannot breathe. Should this happen, try:

- Sniffing in through the nose (like smelling a flower), then blowing out through pursed lips (blowing out a candle)—this allows some back pressure to reopen the stuck vocal folds.
- You could also try putting the tongue on the bottom of your mouth behind your bottom teeth.

Recovery positions
- Stand with your chest open and your hands on your hips or on your head.
- Bend over with your hands on your knees.

Long-term breathing re-education is essential, often in conjunction with seeing a speech language therapist.

Top tips for anyone with a vocal problem

- Always start with breathing retraining (see chapter 8).
- Try the sniff test (see box entitled "SNIFF TEST").
- Take a nose belly breath as you start to speak, then take in small

sips of air through your mouth as you finish your sentence.

- Practise reading out loud, mindful of commas, full stops and syllables.

Another important aspect of speech and voice is being able to express oneself. As a clinician I have learnt to listen, as each patient has a story. For the true healing to occur, the story often needs to be revealed.

A top secondary school rower, Sarah presented initially with neck pain and incredible discomfort in her upper chest. She was in her final year at school and was unable to go to the national championships, which had long been her dream, as a result of injury. She had seen her usual musculoskeletal physiotherapist for treatment of the discomfort, but it was not shifting.

Sarah's story highlights how emotion can present as physical discomfort. During her session, we managed to get her to relax and achieve a baseline calm state, a place she had not been in for some time. At this point in the treatment, she broke down in tears and admitted she was grief-stricken and angry that she was not at the national championships. After this, her discomfort and pain subsided—she literally needed to get the emotion off her chest.

Summary

- Being heard is a basic human need.
- Breathing is the foundation of good voice production.
- Voice is created when air hits the vocal folds.
- Voice and expression enhance confidence both at work and socially.

CHAPTER 13

COUGH, HOICK AND SPIT

Respiratory conditions and disorders

Perhaps you know someone with a chronic cough—maybe it's that person in the office who is always coughing or it's you when the air is cold or you've had a chest infection. Everyone knows someone with a lung issue such as asthma, frequent chest infections or a rattly, wheezy chest. It might be mild, occasional disease, or they might be struggling for breath, drowning in too much phlegm, or coughing until they pee their pants or vomit.

It is not much fun living with a respiratory-based disorder or disease. The essence of this chapter is to assure anyone with respiratory disease, disorder or symptoms that there is much that can be done alongside medication.

Healthy breathing practices can enhance and prolong quality of life. If you require assistance, seek one of the skilled medical practitioners working in this field. I cannot sing the praises of cardio-respiratory physiotherapists highly enough—they are the unsung heroes of this chapter.

According to the Global Initiative for Chronic Obstructive Lung Disease (GOLD), in 2019:

- 65 million people suffer from chronic obstructive pulmonary disease (COPD) and 3 million die from it each year. This makes it the third most common cause of death worldwide.
- Pneumonia kills millions of people each year, making it a leading cause of death in the very young and very old.
- 91 per cent of the world's population live in places where air quality exceeds the WHO's safe guidelines.
- 334 million people suffer from asthma, making it the most common chronic disease of childhood. It affects 14 per cent of

children globally and this number is rising.

The basic principles of the assessment and treatment of the breathing pattern disorders that commonly accompany lung conditions are common to all, with specific considerations applying to some.

There are many other respiratory conditions which may be combinations of the above diseases or other diseases, such as cystic fibrosis, adult respiratory distress syndrome (ARDS) and sarcoidosis. For the purposes of this chapter, the main ones covered will be COPD, asthma and bronchiectasis. I will not discuss medication, as this is best left to your GP.

For more information on asthma, *Dynamic Breathing for Asthma* is an excellent little handbook (see RESOURCES).

Lung disease can affect:

- the airways, as seen in asthma
- alveoli, which are the air sacs at the end of the air passages, as seen in emphysema

- the interstitium, which is the lung tissue that supports the airways, lymph and blood vessels in place, where the oxygen and carbon dioxide exchange from the lungs into the blood stream occurs, as seen in pneumonia and sarcoidosis
- the blood vessels, as seen in the pulmonary embolisms (blood clots) caused by COVID-19
- the pleura, the lining between the lung and chest wall, as seen in pleurisy.

Chronic obstructive pulmonary disease (COPD)

This is a group of progressive lung diseases that affect and reduce airflow. The most common ones are emphysema, chronic asthma and chronic bronchitis.

Emphysema

Emphysema destroys the air sacs (alveoli) in your lungs. This then interferes with airflow and increases the resistance to movement of the air in and out of the lungs. Often trapping air, it will feel like the lungs are too full of air, so it's like trying to breathe at the very top of an in breath.

As emphysema progresses, some air just can't be breathed out. However, by addressing your breathing pattern, you can make sure you are doing everything you can to help. (See PURSED-LIPPED EXHALE BREATHING.)

Chronic bronchitis

Bronchitis is a condition where there is inflammation of the lining of your bronchial tubes, which are the tubes that carry air to and from the lungs. This inflammation stops the cilia from working and allows mucus to build up. This might be caused by an infection, or by exposure to irritants such as smoke or air pollutants.

Asthma

Asthma is a chronic inflammatory disorder in the airways of the lungs. The airways become overactive and tighten, and then can become inflamed. This makes it harder to breathe in and out, bringing with it a sensation like that of breathing through a straw.

Air can also get trapped, which causes hyperinflation to occur. This means not enough air is exhaled, often leading to upper-chest breathing and the emergency muscles doing all the work of breathing. It's no wonder the feeling of breathlessness is all too common among people with asthma. These episodes may reverse on their own or in response to treatment/medication.

The triggers of asthma are many and varied, but if it is well controlled you shouldn't experience any symptoms.

The Asthma Control Test (ACT) has been proven to be useful for assessing whether asthma is well managed or not. You can find this test online at www.a sthmacontroltest.com.

How does asthma work?

Mast cells are like watchdogs lying in the tissues supporting the airways. They give warning signals to the airways, and when they feel threatened they will activate higher histamine levels in the blood, which triggers broncho-constriction (tight pipes) and swelling of the airway linings. This is the lungs' attempt to keep foreign invaders, such as dust, bacteria and viruses, from entering the airways. However, with asthma, the airway has become hypersensitive and many usually unthreatening things can trigger a response—for example, the pollen from a flower, or exposure to mould.

It is important to know that the airways will also tighten in response to lower blood CO_2 levels. Even if there is no environmental trigger such as cat dander or pollen, if someone who has asthma is breathing in a way that lowers their CO_2 level, such as breathing through the mouth and upper chest at rest, this can cause airway tightening even in the absence of an allergic trigger.

Anna is 48 and she presented with a history of well-managed asthma. She had a persistent cough, which was worse at night, causing poor sleep. She was experiencing frequent headaches. She had an upper-chest breathing pattern and was mouth breathing.

Treatment initially involved a nasal hygiene regime, followed by breathing retraining at rest and practising a two-minute calm-down, bliss-out before sleep. This treatment then progressed to breathing cadence with movement, plus the introduction of inspiratory muscle training.

Within a week Anna's sleep had improved, and within three weeks her persistent cough was under control.

Bronchiectasis

Bronchiectasis is chronic irreversible damage to the airways often due to severe lung infections or inhaled material, which can cause dilatation and distortions to the affected airways and their linings. The ciliary function is destroyed, which makes the clearance of mucus difficult. If mucus is not moved regularly, it becomes the prime site for bacteria to flourish.

Note: There are various stages in all of these diseases, from mild to severe.

Treatment

For all of these conditions, the following treatment plan is recommended:
- basic breathing retraining
- the active cycle of breathing technique (ACBT) as the first line of defence for anyone who has problems moving mucus.

Clearing sputum

Clearing sputum (the respiratory name for mucus) from the lungs is essential. Sputum is produced in the nasal cavity and in the airways. Its function is to protect the linings of the respiratory system and to keep them moist. It also traps particles that can cause harm, such as bacteria, dust and smoke.

Sputum is moved by hair-like projections called cilia, which work in a sweeping motion to mobilise the sputum out of the lungs, where it is then either swallowed or spat out. If the cilia or the linings are damaged, this sputum can become stagnant in the lungs. This is *not* ideal, as infection can set in causing the patient to become unwell.

Sputum clearance devices can be used to help clear the lungs and airways of mucus. They work by creating pressure, which helps move the sputum, and vibrations, which loosen the mucus in the airway (see section entitled "Sputum clearance devices"). Speak with your physiotherapist to find out which device best suits you. They will also be able to show you the correct techniques for using these devices.

A cardio-respiratory physiotherapist's tool kit includes fitness regimes and strategies to help with breathlessness, chronic coughing and moving sputum.

You can try some of the suggestions below or those found on the websites recommended in section entitled "Sputum clearance devices". I strongly recommend that you also have at least one one-on-one session with a skilled health professional.

Always have tissues with you to spit into, and put them straight into the bin when you've finished coughing. Don't leave them lying around and don't forget to wash your hands.

Huffing

Huffing is breathing in a similar way to breathing on a mirror to fog it up. This helps to move secretions in your airways by keeping the airways splinted open and thus allowing the sputum to move up and out. A huff uses less energy than coughing and is more effective.

Drink plenty of fluids

Drinking approximately six to eight cups of fluid every day is required. Water, juice, teas and coffees all count. If you do not drink *enough,* it can cause the sputum to get thicker, and more difficult to cough up.

Steam inhalation

This helps to moisten the upper airway, and for some people it can help make clearing sputum easier. It can also be helpful for those who have sinus infections.

• Boil water in a pot or the jug.

- Allow to cool for a few minutes; be cautious with the heat.
- Add Vicks VapoRub, Friar's Balsam or eucalyptus oil to the water for added punch.
- Use a paper bag as a funnel over a bowl of the hot water.
- Put your mouth at the other end of the paper bag and breathe in and out. (You could also use a towel over your head, but the paper bag can feel less claustrophobic.)

Other options

Breath stacking for assistance to remove sputum

Breath stacking is when a breath is not fully exhaled before another breath is taken in, so stacking one breath upon another. Fill the lungs then hold for another four to six seconds, before blowing out using a pursed-lipped exhale.

There are various devices that can be used to assist this process. When used, they cause vibration in the airways on the out breath, which helps to shift sputum (see section entitled "Airflow control").

ACTIVE CYCLE OF BREATHING TECHNIQUE (ACBT)

This clearance technique is a key treatment taught by physiotherapists. To ensure you are doing it correctly, I suggest you see your cardio-respiratory therapist for a session then use the notes below to remind you of the sequence.

The technique alternates between relaxed abdominal breaths and big breaths. Then it finishes with what is called a 'huff', also known as a forced expiratory technique (FET).

You can do this sitting, standing or lying down, depending on what works best for you.

• Take two breaths doing relaxed abdominal nose (deep, not big) breathing.

• Take two full (big) breaths, filling the chest gently via the nose.

• Hold for two to three seconds.

- Let go so the air whooshes quietly out of your chest through your mouth.
- Repeat this cycle three or four times.
- Try two huffs (see huff explanation in section entitled "Huffing"). Only perform one or two huffs together, as repeatedly huffing can make your chest tight.
- The volume of the huff will depend on where the mucus is.
- If the sputum is in the top of the lungs, take in a big breath and open your mouth wide and huff out quickly.
- If the sputum is in the bottom of the lungs, take a normal-sized breath, then huff out. You could also gently tighten your belly at the end of the breath to ensure the air is fully out and you have reached the lower, deeper airway.
- If you can hear a rattle or feel any mucus, cough no more than twice to bring it out.
- If it is still stuck, don't keep coughing. Instead, repeat the cycle

until it becomes easier to cough up the sputum.

- Repeat the cycle until the huff sounds dry.
- Always finish with relaxed abdominal nose breathing.

This is a simple way of keeping ahead of mucus production and helping prevent chest infections. This is the basic method, but a face-to-face session with a respiratory physiotherapist will enable you to make it more specific for you and your lungs.

Back tapping

Having someone tap your back is an added bonus. By gently vibrating the chest wall, they help loosen mucus build-up while also relieving muscle tension. Children especially enjoy this and, as ACBT is sometimes difficult for children to perform, it can be another option for them if it's done carefully. Try doing some gentle massage as well.

Kids often prefer the more active approach, and they appreciate the physical touch and attention, particularly if they have been frightened by their symptoms.

Sputum is perfectly normal

Some people find the whole notion of chest clearance disgusting and cannot/will not cough up sputum. Swallowing it is perfectly normal and younger children tend to do this. However, excessive sputum is better out than in.

Coughing it up also provides us with an opportunity to quickly check to see what colour the phlegm is. Pale cream or yellowy hues usually indicate allergic or inflammatory responses, while darker or greenish tones and an unpleasant taste are likely to be the result of an infection.

Doctors often like to send a sputum sample for investigation to make sure the right sort of antibiotic is chosen for the particular type of bug. This helps reduce the risk of having to take repeated courses of antibiotics if the first one fails to work. Take care to complete each course of antibiotics and contact your doctor immediately if you experience a bad reaction.

Chronic cough

A chronic cough is one that lasts longer than four months. Note that coughing is protective and can be good. A cough can alert us to a problem.

Some of the reasons for a chronic cough are respiratory disease, reflux, post-nasal drip, larynx problems such as vocal cord dysfunction, cysts, and the post-viral chronic cough cycle.

Treatment will depend on the cause, so see your GP if your cough lasts longer than four months.

In the interim, here are a few tips to help:
- nose breathe
- breathe low and slow in your chest, at low volumes.
- sip plenty of water
- suppress the desire to cough by swallowing hard, dropping your shoulders and concentrating on breathing out.

Nose blowing

If done too violently, blowing your nose can damage the tubes that connect with the inner ear, causing sinus and ear problems. The best way to blow your nose is to block off one nostril while clearing the other gently. This is especially important for young children.

Breathing retraining and other therapies

The initial breathing retraining goals are similar to those in chapter 8:

- Check your body tension.
- Is your nose clear?
- Is the abdomen gently rising and falling when you breathe?

The treatment then follows that of chapter 8, with some amendments. First, you may wish to start in a sitting position. Check your breathing and body tension in an upright position. This helps to limit any breathless sensations that may be experienced when lying down. The goal is to ensure that breathing is slow, low and rhythmical, and through the nose when possible.

Pursed-lipped breathing

With COPD, the diaphragm becomes less able to move as the lungs puff up and become hyperinflated, so it contributes less to the work of breathing. The neck and shoulder muscles take over and frequently become tight and tense and sore. You can breathe out through your mouth if this is easier. The best way to do this is called a pursed-lipped exhale.

This is a beneficial technique for anyone, in particular those with emphysema. It involves breathing in through the nose and out through puckered lips, as if you are blowing out a candle. This slows down your pace of breathing and prolongs the out breath compared to the in breath. This helps reduce the amount of air trapped in the lungs.

It also serves to create back pressure in the airway, which produces a small amount of what is called positive end-expiratory pressure (PEEP). This helps with opening and stabilising collapsed or unstable alveoli.

This opening of the alveoli improves gas exchange and helps reduce breathlessness. It is very useful during any activity that can cause breathlessness, such as walking up inclines or stairs, through to cycling up a steep hill.

PURSED-LIPPED BREATHING EXERCISE

- Relax your neck and shoulders.
- Keeping your mouth closed, breathe in through your nose.
- Then pucker or purse your lips as though you were going to whistle or blow out a candle.
- Breathe out slowly by blowing air through your pursed lips.
- Then try and breathe back in through your nose and repeat the pursed-lipped exhale.
- Repeat for a couple of cycles until you feel your breathing is under control.

Pursed-lipped exhale acts to:
- relieve shortness of breath by slowing the breath rate

- keeps the airways open longer, which decreases the work that goes into breathing
- improves ventilation by moving old air (CO_2) trapped in the lungs out and making room for new, fresh oxygen.

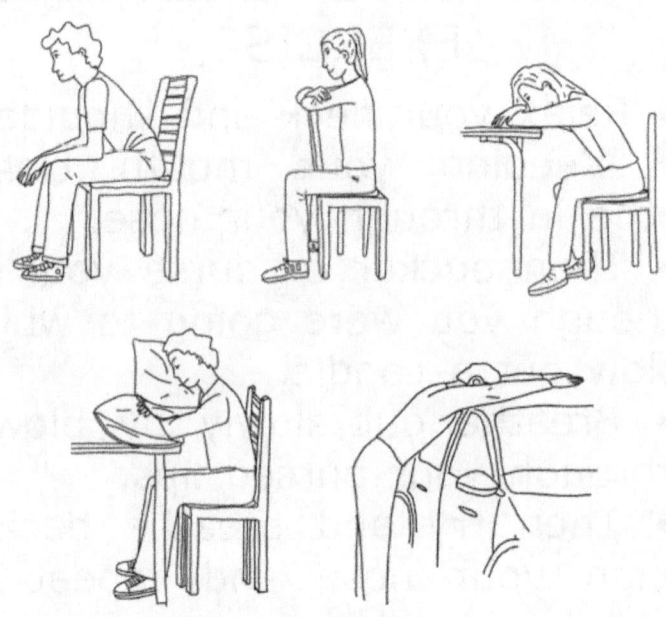

Recovery or rest positions

These are beneficial for saving energy and for recovery when breathless. The postures stop the oxygen-hungry upper-chest muscles working so much and help assist with abdominal breathing. When in these postures, try to regulate your breathing by focusing on the out breath. Try pursed-lipped breathing. Let the in breath just happen how it wants to.

Pacing and exercise

Energy conservation, energy-efficient resting positions, co-ordinating movement, and breathing well can reduce breathlessness and conserve energy.

In particular with COPD, it is normal to have to start breathing using your mouth when exercising or walking up inclines, especially stairs. When doing exercise, remember to be aware of your breathing and pace the breath to your movements.

Awareness of breathing and remembering not to hold your breath when exercising will make a difference to your ability to move well and help with endurance. (See paced breathing exercises.)

Positive expiratory pressure (PEP) therapy

This simply means applying a pressure or resistance when breathing out. This pressure helps to open the airways, which allows the sputum to move up with more ease. There are many different devices on the market to use for PEP (see section entitled "Sputum clearance devices"). Your respiratory physiotherapist will help you to select the device that is most effective for your disorder. For example, someone with COPD may require a different device to a person with bronchiectasis.

Inspiratory muscle training (IMT)

Inspiratory (in breath) muscles are prone to over-use during acute asthma episodes or as a result of fatigue and deconditioning. IMT devices target the diaphragm (see section entitled "Inspiratory Muscle Training"). Asthma sufferers who have used these devices report a reduction in medication use and fewer hospital visits. They also note the added bonus of improved exercise tolerance and fitness.

For those with COPD, there is conclusive evidence that IMT improves inspiratory muscle function (strength and endurance), decreases symptoms of dyspnoea and improves exercise capacity.

Emma is 47 and has had asthma all her life. After a bad winter, when she was plagued with chest infections and worsening asthma, she got into a cycle of decline. She lost a lot of fitness and found she couldn't mow the lawns or do other things she'd normally do.

She was prescribed with repeat courses of prednisone and antibiotics, but these left her feeling worse. She gained weight as she couldn't exercise because of shortness of breath, which she said scared her a bit.

Eventually, Emma saw a chest specialist, who suggested some breathing re-education. Her shoulder muscles were like rocks and locked into breathing high into her chest. When this was pointed out to her, Emma couldn't believe it as she'd been totally unaware of her neck and chest. Her breathing rate was 24 breaths a minute, which was twice as fast as normal. Her peak flow was 340, which was lower than it should be.

Emma was encouraged to use a Powerbreathe, which she took to easily. As it only took a couple of minutes morning and evening, it wasn't a chore for her. Within two weeks, she reported feeling an enormous improvement. Her peak flow went up to 370 and her Ventolin consumption went right down.

After eight weeks, her peak flow was up to 450. The breathing retraining and diaphragm strengthening had also helped her to turn a corner. According to Emma, 'In all my years as an asthmatic, 30-odd years, I had never received any help with breathing. The emphasis was always *on medication. I know I can't do without my puffers, and I know breathing better doesn't cure my asthma, but my quality of life has improved out of sight. I can exercise comfortably, I'm much fitter, my weight has dropped, and I enjoy mowing the lawn again!'*

Finally, if you are having an episode of asthma or a COPD exacerbation, follow your GP's advice. Use your medication and use your crisis plan.

A note on allergies

People with allergies often have many episodes of sinus infections, hayfever, viral infections, and common colds. Breathing well and nasal hygiene are essential for keeping the immune system strong and the body healthy.

It's well documented that disordered breathing, especially over-breathing, lowers CO_2 which causes the mast cells to release histamine more easily and increases circulating histamine levels in the blood. This acts as a trigger to asthma and allergies. If you tend to over-breathe, this may predispose you to allergies or wheezing, so ensure daily practice of your healthy breathing techniques as seen in chapter 8.

There are also some other things that may help if you have allergies:

- Try to detect your allergen.
- Remember that if you are run-down and tired, you are more susceptible to reacting to whatever you are allergic to, so get plenty of sleep and eat regularly.
- Take medications as prescribed.
- Breathe well to maintain health and a strong immune system and to avoid over-production of histamine.
- Exercise for the above reasons.
- Maintain a low-allergy environment.

Summary

- Lung disease requires medical attention.
- Self-care can make a big difference.
- Key aspects of self-care are:
  - understanding your disease

  - understanding your medications and using them effectively

– clearing sputum effectively

– using your breathing pattern and rest positions to help avoidable breathlessness

– pursed-lipped breathing, which is particularly relevant with lung disease.

- If you want advice that is tailored to you, your lungs and your lifestyle, see a respiratory physiotherapist.
- Awareness of breathing can help for many reasons—energy conservation, improved quality of life and longevity.
- Rest positions are beneficial for saving energy.
- Sputum clearance should be something that is incorporated into your everyday routine if sputum is an issue for you.
- Inspiratory muscle training is beneficial to all those with lung disease.

CHAPTER 14

PERSISTENT PAIN, CHRONIC FATIGUE SYNDROME AND SLEEP DISORDERS

For most of us, when we injure ourselves we're sore for a few days, then after a few days or weeks pain will subside. But for some, whose initial injuries appeared to be no different, their pain can last for years. These persistent-pain patients make up a big proportion of the client base we see in the clinic.

There are many causes of pain and many types of pain, but the basic principles apply regardless of whether the pain lasts a short time or a long time, if it is dull, sharp or throbbing, and whether it's caused by poor ergonomics, tension, bad posture, injury or disease.

Pain is very much an individual experience and should always be respected and taken seriously.

The International Association for the Study of Pain (IASP) defines pain as 'an unpleasant sensory and emotional experience associated with, or resembling that associated with, actual or potential tissue damage'.

Our understanding of pain and persistent pain has progressed massively in the past few decades. It is complex, but we know that pain does not have to be associated with any tissue damage. Often, a vicious belief cycle is set up and physiological changes occur in the body as a result. Breathing pattern disorders are common, as a natural response to pain is to wince and breath-hold in protection. Sleep disturbances are also common when people are in pain, as are anxiety, depression and low moods.

John is 55. He has a long history of persistent, severe, lower-back pain. He's had it so long that he can't remember what his initial trigger was. As a result, John had adapted many protective postures and protective movements. His gut was held tight and tense 'to protect his back', causing him to breathe into his upper chest and to overuse his neck and shoulder muscles, which were often painful. His breaths were short and sharp, and he would wince when he walked. His X-rays were clear. All treatments to date had only helped temporarily.

John's treatment included education, breathing and relaxation, and breathing re-education. Breathing pattern retraining was encouraged for John, initially at a minimum of twice daily, along with green dot reminders throughout the day. This formed a major part of John's rehabilitation.

Once he had a good understanding of this, we introduced breathing and healthier movement patterns, and movement cadence. When this had been achieved, he was referred to colleagues for gym rehabilitation.

Within weeks, John had started to move more and better. He relaxed physically, which helped with his sleep. His pain was still present, but it was not dominating his life as much as it had, and he felt he could control it more.

What John found unbelievable was that by physically relaxing, not bracing and moving more freely, his pain levels decreased significantly.

Education

One of the key principles is education, so that the individual understands the concept of pain. Many people have a distorted belief system surrounding pain, and unless it is understood, it can be hard to motivate some to change their behaviour. The main belief that needs to be challenged is that pain is associated with injury, damage or harm. However, pain does not necessarily mean tissue, disc or joint damage. There are many factors that play into the pathways and psyche of pain, such as beliefs, genetics, and social and cultural influences.

Fear is a major emotional behaviour, so it might help to know some facts and figures about it. Only 1 per cent of back pain is actually associated with an organic medical cause.

Pain education is not dissimilar to the education used for breathlessness. It is an individual experienced sensation, and many factors feed into it. As such, a team approach to treatment is often best to get you on the road to recovery. Please seek help early if you feel you have a problem.

There are many excellent resources available for those in severe pain. I highly recommend the podcast series *Empowered Beyond Pain* by Professor Peter O'Sullivan.

Breathing and relaxation

Often patients with chronic pain are unaware of the amount of tension they carry and they often have poor body awareness. Therefore, regular and focused use of the relaxation response, body scans and basic breathing awareness is important. This helps to reduce mental and physical stress. People often present, as John did, with massive protective postures. In his case, holding his gut tensely to protect his back and moving in a very robotic fashion.

Abdominal, pelvic or lower-back pain frequently involves splinting of the abdominal muscles. This results in pushing breathing up into the upper chest, thereby recruiting the energy-hungry upper-chest muscles. This process creates dysfunction and results in poor tissue health. Muscles do not move as they should, so deconditioning occurs, leading to further loss of muscle mass.

Poor breathing patterns result in decreased oxygenation of cells and tissues as well as changes at the nerve synapse, which in turn lead to poor nerve–muscle messaging and decreased efficiency in muscle fibre recruitment. All of this adds to the pain cycle.

Altered breathing at rest is the ultimate driver for the red zone and stress chemicals, so it's no wonder it can make you feel bad. Alongside education comes awareness of these protective postures. The introduction of progressive muscle relaxation exercises (see section entitled "Relaxation training exercises"), quick body scans (see section entitled "A quick, relaxing body scan") and knowing how to loosen and let go are all big steps for many pain sufferers.

Breathing re-education

A breathing pattern disorder will exacerbate pain, not just mechanically, but also at a cellular and nerve-pathway level. When we over-breathe, this drives us into the red zone and our CO_2 levels drop. Both of these lower our pain threshold, meaning pain will be amplified. So breathing well not only benefits us mechanically, but also helps us to achieve baseline calm.

People with chronic pain often come to the clinic having tried a huge cocktail of medications, which can have their own side effects. The techniques outlined in chapter eight are extremely attractive options to those who want to learn non-drug-based pain-management techniques or reduce existing medications.

Chronic fatigue syndrome, post-viral malaise and COVID-19

For many years, we have seen people present with chronic fatigue syndrome (CFS). Medically, the cause of CFS is unknown, but it is believed that viruses, stress, a compromised nervous system and hormone imbalances can contribute to it. There are certain viruses that have been associated with chronic fatigue such as Epstein-Barr virus (EBV) and human herpesvirus 6 and more recently COVID-19. There is no accurate diagnostic test for CFS, but lingering overwhelming fatigue for more than four to six months is a good indicator.

The common symptom to all is extreme fatigue after physical or mental activities. This is known as post-exertional malaise (PEM).

Other common symptoms are:
- muscle and joint pain
- headaches
- dizziness
- lack of clarity of thought (brain fog)

- problems thinking, remembering or focusing
- difficulty regulating blood pressure and heart rate.

Symptoms are reported to come and go, so awareness and a lot of listening to the body are vital. A symptom not commonly listed, but that I've noted from clinical experience, is that of anxiety—worry, low mood associated with health, 'Will I recover?', 'What is actually happening to me?', 'People think this is all in my head', 'What about my job and my family?', 'I can't function'.

Often these have been active busy people who are suddenly bed-bound and totally incapacitated, so it's no wonder they feel anxious.

Rehabilitation involves many health specialists, from physiotherapists to dieticians, occupational therapists to medical specialists. The important thing to know is that lots can be done, and you can be guided through recovery. Seek help. (See resources, in particular the paced breathing exercises.)

The term 'long Covid' has been assigned to patients who display these symptoms for months after contracting COVID-19. This is reported to occur in 10 per cent of people who've had the virus. This group experience symptoms for one, two or even three months or more after they were infected.

When the body adapts metabolically to fight a virus or cold, or protect us against threat, our breathing will change to match this. There can be an increase in speed (respiratory rate), or an increase or decrease in volume. When we experience an increase in temperature, our respiratory rate increases in order to maintain the pH and internal balance of the body. But, once this threat is removed the altered pattern often remains, so breathing is dysfunctional, resulting in breathing pattern disorder.

Other factors come into play, especially in COVID-19, as it is a respiratory-based virus that can attack lung tissue, and individuals may be left with irreparable lung damage (see lung diseases in chapter 11).

The experience of breathlessness, chronic cough and general body deconditioning all play a part. The first step in rehabilitation is to look at breathing patterns. However, it must be noted that everyone presents as an individual case and should be seen by a health care professional for a structured rehabilitation programme.

Jill, 57, has had chronic fatigue syndrome for over 20 years. She has learnt to live with the condition but still experiences fatigue, sleep disturbance and post exertional malaise. In her words: 'When I really relax properly and focus on my breathing, my body goes into a different state. It's just that I am constantly fighting fatigue and pain, which takes a lot of energy. In my relaxation I can melt away the pain and it doesn't require any energy.'

Factors that need to be addressed

Mechanical dysfunction

Often the breathing pattern has changed from a nose abdominal breathing pattern at rest, to that of upper chest and mouth at rest.

Muscle deconditioning

The decrease in diaphragmatic force can be reduced from 20 per cent to more than 50 per cent. This alteration can occur within 12 hours, especially if someone has been ventilated. The diaphragm is the vital pump in the body, pumping oxygen to all cells in the body. Inspiratory muscle training will help restore correct motor patterns and muscle health. It is essential to start this slowly and very cautiously, so as not to fatigue the muscles or further reinforce poor patterns.

Biochemistry

Often dysfunctional breathing mantains lowered CO_2 levels. Spending too long in this state can compromise the bicarbonate buffer, which is a chemical process that works to maintain pH in the blood. This often becomes depleted (see section entitled "The chemical advantages of breathing well"). This means that when we move, the normal process of clearing lactic acid doesn't work very quickly, so the muscles fatigue prematurely, leading to aches and pains similar to those normally associated with strenuous exercise. This is the basis of the extreme premature ache felt in muscles, and CO_2 needs to be restored. How we breathe is an active way of biochemically restoring the balance. This is important, and it highlights why breathing is a critical part of rehabilitation for anyone who experiences chronic fatigue syndrome, long covid or muscle aches post exertion.

Anxiety and worry

Confusion over symptoms, worry about your health and the lack of recovery are common.

Pacing

This chemical blowout, and the body working as if it has run a marathon even if you've just walked to the kitchen, can result in sore muscles, achy joints and exhaustion. Pacing with breathing co-ordination and movement is essential.

For people with these conditions, the 'push through it' attitude *will not work.* Pushing through will further inflame the system and, chances are, a day in bed will follow.

> How we breathe is an active way of biochemically restoring the balance.

I suggest to my clients that they think of energy in units or like a bank account. I tell them to use just 10 spoons of energy a day. Once these spoons have been used, they are gone. The body resembles a bank account, so if you overspend energy, you will find yourself in overdraft. If there is no money in the bank and you are in overdraft, the only way is to repay the debt and accumulate more money. In this case, instead of money, you need to accumulate more energy. This is why recovery is a long, gradual process; it is literally step by step.

Paced activities and movements should be carried out in small, manageable, bite-sized blocks with rest breaks in between. Monitoring heart rate often and co-ordinating breathing well to stay under the anerobic threshold will keep your physiology balanced. More than ever, listening to the body is imperative. It's OK to edge into tiredness but *not* into fatigue. Pushing too hard will lead to exhaustion. (See the pacing suggestions in section entitled "Pacing and cadence".)

This is all about energy conservation, so remember if your breathing rate speeds up so does the amount of energy you use.

Sleep preparation—skills not pills

The way you breathe during your day will have an impact on how you breathe at night. The first step to sleeping well is to breathe well (see chapter 8).

I cannot emphasise enough how important it is to do a calm-down, bliss-out exercise when in bed. Even though I would like to think of myself as a queen of calm, I still do this every night and every morning. It sets the scene for sleep and it sets the scene for the day ahead.

Some other tips to help improve your sleep

- Try to make your bedroom a peaceful, electronic-free zone.
- Reduce extremes of mental stimulation an hour before bed.
- Have a warm (not hot) bath or shower before bed.
- Being overheated delays the release of melatonin needed to induce sleep, so keep cool.
- Wear bed socks if your feet feel cold, and if your feet feel hot, put them out from under the covers. Our feet are an important part of our temperature regulation mechanism.
- Alcohol may promote sleep onset, but can lead to sleep that is poor, fragmented and unrefreshing.
- Reduce stimulants. Avoid coffee after 3pm.
- Switch off electronics before sleep. Devices emit large amounts of blue light, and exposure to this prior to sleep prevents melatonin from being released. However, blue light during

the day is good as it helps maintain the circadian rhythm (sleep/wake rhythm).

Summary

Pain

- Back pain can be caused by many factors.
- Pain does not necessarily stem from harm, hurt or injury.
- Pain can lead to altered postures and breathing patterns.
- Breathing pattern disorders will exacerbate pain. When we over-breathe, this can drive us into the red zone, lowering the pain threshold and amplifying pain.
- There is a three-step treatment plan for pain:
    - education and understanding of pain
    - body awareness
    - breathing re-education.

Chronic fatigue

Breathing has a direct relationship to energy expenditure.

The rate, rhythm, depth and flow of our breathing will determine the quality and quantity of energy we use.

Key ingredients of recovery are:
- pacing
- units of energy
- breathing re-education.

Treat energy like a bank account. Work in units of energy, and figure out the amount that is safe to use daily.

Sleep

- The key to healthy sleep depends on stress levels throughout the day, so self-check often—use the green dot method to tune in.
- Calm-down bliss-outs and body-scan breathing are essential pre-sleep.
- Set the scene for healthy sleep.

CHAPTER 15

IGNITING THE LIFE FORCE

A M□ORI PERSPECTIVE BY JOLIE DAVIS

Introducing Jolie

Beyond the body, mind and chemistry lies the magic of unseen energy. The lens on breathing through which this book is written is one of Western medicine. My background in physical education, physiotherapy and mind–body medicine, as well as writing from New Zealand European descent, leans to the narrative of Western thinking. As I am a New Zealander, I must also include the perspective of breathing from a Māori perspective as Māori are the tangata whenua, the indigenous people of New Zealand.

Jolie is a respected kaimirimiri, a practitioner of mirimiri, traditional Māori bodywork and healing. Her journey began when she received mirimiri treatment as a young mother struggling to find peace with her past. She learnt that without personal healing for herself, her pain would likely be passed on to the next generation. This was her first lesson in mirimiri and romiromi.

Later, while working as a nurse in the health system, Jolie realised she could offer much more in the healing process, and this drove her to return to her traditional roots.

A Māori perspective

Ko Maunga Piko te maunga → Maunga Piko is my mountain

Ko Pārengarenga te moana → Pārengarenga harbour is my ocean

Ko Ngāti Kurī te iwi → Ngāti Kurī is my tribe

Ko Ngāti Murukaharā te hapū→ Ngāti Murukaharā is my subtribe

Ko Rewiri Hongi te tupuna → Rewiri Hongi is my ancestor

Ko Jolie Davis tōku ingoa → My name is Jolie Davis

Te hā

The breath, life force, life essence—te hā is all of these things.

One of my teachers taught me that the breath is so important to us (Māori) that it is considered even more important than aroha. He would say, 'You try holding your breath and having loving thoughts and see which one you give up first!'

We laughed at this saying, but I never forgot. That was the first time I realised the importance of breathing. We must breathe in order to experience life and well-being.

From a cultural perspective, we talk about how, when a baby is being born, it transitions from one state to another, from the world of becoming to the world of light—ki te whai ao, ki te ao mārama.

On entering the physical realm, the first thing the baby does is take a breath. This is known as the breath of life. Tihei wā mauri ora!

From that point on, we continue to breathe until we take our last breath and return home to our tūpuna, our ancestors, in the spiritual realms.

When we formally meet someone for the first time, we hongi (press noses/foreheads together) and breathe in deeply. We are doing this to share breath with each other and, in doing so, connect and share our life essence with that person.

Traditional practitioners of mirimiri and romiromi are taught to breathe in a specific way while working. We understand the importance of breathing, which connects the practitioner to the whaiora, the person receiving healing or treatment. They are encouraged to breathe deeply and not to hold the breath, especially when experiencing intense pain. This assists the body to release what is being held at a cellular level. Controlled and intentional breathing also helps to raise awareness and connection within their own bodies, which is vital to achieving and maintaining wellness.

These days I see and treat a lot of 'disconnection' with people who come to me for treatment. I see the tightness in the chest and shoulders, the frozen diaphragms, the locked ribcages, the shallow breathing that manifests in low oxygen in the blood and body, causing chronic tiredness, headaches and panic/anxiety in the mind and body.

First, I release the tension in the body, deeply working into the diaphragm and chest. Then they must re-learn how to breathe properly. For many, the disconnection is a result of trauma disrupting the central nervous system and/or respiratory system, or they have learnt to survive by holding the breath in.

Diminished breathing = diminished life force/life essence

The haka (*Ha*/ka): To ignite the breath or to ignite the life force. This is one of the reasons for performing the haka.

Aroha (Aro/*ha*): To direct life force/breath/essence towards others. Aroha also talks about how we direct our intention (aro) using the breath.

A simple breathing exercise
Eight seconds in-breath.

Eight seconds hold.
Eight seconds exhale.
Breathe.

Breathing properly from the puku/diaphragm, not the chest, detoxifies the body and releases 'stale air' from the puku and lungs. As a result, the body is energised, and the nervous system calmed.

These days, the problem is we sit too much for too long, we hold the puku in and push the chest out, and we are exposed to a lot of stress that causes our bodies and our muscles to freeze and the breathing to change.

The Atua Tāwhirimātea is commonly known as the Atua/God of Wind because his breath is the hau or wind. Within Nature, different winds arrive at specific times of the month or season to cleanse and clear the environment. It is the same process for the human body.

In Te Ao Māori, we also understand that we breathe through the soles of our feet! This is what we know as true full-body breathing. The in breath happens there, and we draw energy up through the body to the crown and exhale back down to the soles of the feet, and clear/cleanse our systems this way. This is just as important as the physical breath that we take with our lungs, if not more so.

The teachers who taught me would say 'Take off your shoes and socks—you are suffocating your body!' This is something I am always aware of and teach all the time.

Breathing is not just a mechanical process of the body. It is the vital exchange of essence and energy with the natural environment around us, which revitalises, energises and clears all systems. Connectedness is vital with regard to wellness.

The easiest way to connect the mental, spiritual and physical aspects all at the same time is simply to breathe.

Tihei wāmauri ora!

EXERCISES AND OTHER STRATEGIES

Emergency strategies

The most important technique for emergency breathing when acutely panicking, hyperventilating or over-breathing is the BradCliff Five by Fives exercise. This can be followed with some grounding exercises to bring you into the present moment.

BradCliff Five by Fives for recovery breathing

Prolonged over-breathing quickly depletes the body of CO_2. This can cause distressing symptoms like tingling fingertips or lips, light-headedness, poor balance or panicky/nauseous feelings. If you experience this, try this effective and discreet way of restoring CO_2 levels that places you in control.

1. Cup both hands over your nose and mouth.

2. Breathe softly in and out through the nose (if you can, otherwise use your mouth) five times.
3. Drop your hands to your lap and count to five.
4. Repeat breathing with cupped hands, counting each breath in and out, up to five again.
5. Repeat this five by five sequence until the symptoms subside.

Grounding exercises

This is an excellent exercise to use in all stress-out situations. The aim of it is to bring awareness to the present moment to distract us from our thoughts. It can be done either standing or sitting.

1. Focus on your feet.
2. Feel your toes, heels and the soles of your feet on the ground beneath you.
3. Relax your knees.
4. Drop your shoulders.
5. Focus on your out breath.
6. Now breathe in nose, low and slow.
7. Breathe out.

8. Pause.
9. Feel your feet on the ground and continue what you were doing.

When mind and body recovery is necessary in the middle of a game or sport

This exercise literally involves taking a second to take a breath.

Place your arms in the recovery positions (either with your hands on your knees or on your head) and focus on the horizon. Focusing on the horizon triggers the green zone, the parasympathetic nervous system, whereas focusing on something closer can trigger the sympathetic red zone chain.

1. Stop.
2. Pause.
3. Focus outwards.
4. Feel your feet.
5. Breathe.
6. Pause.
7. Continue what you were doing.

Other physical grounding suggestions

Try these in times of stress, panic or overwhelm.

- Touch or hold on to items near you, focus on them, feel them.
- Put your hands, feet or face in water. Focus on the water's temperature and how it feels. Cold water helps trigger the vagus nerve, which plays a key role in the body's relaxing response.
- Listen to any outside and inside sounds.
- Focus on a colour, then find everything in your line of vision of that colour—for example, all green items.
- Move your body in any way that feels comfortable, and focus on the movements.
- Put a rubber band around one of your wrists and whenever you feel overwhelmed or panic strikes, flick the rubber band. The physical sensation brings you back into your body.

Always try to finish with awareness of feet placement on the ground, pause and breathe out before resuming whatever you were doing.

Relaxation training exercises

Relaxation training covers a spectrum of techniques, but the overall goal is for you to feel looser, freer and less tense physically. This will then help to allow a more effortless, rhythmical and even following breath. These exercises should be integrated into your daily routine to achieve physical awareness of relaxation and breathing well. Just like cleaning your teeth, these exercises should be done daily and for life.

A quick, relaxing body scan

This exercise can be done sitting, standing or lying. Take a few moments to get your body settled.

There is nothing else you need to be doing right now and nowhere else you need to be, so try to stay focused on your body and your breathing—thoughts may come and go and that is fine, just observe them with a gentle curiosity.

Don't forget to breathe. Finish each step with awareness of a breath in and out, then imagine the breath flowing into the body part on which you've just been focusing—for example, your feet, legs, hips or pelvis.

For this exercise, there is no right or wrong. It is all about noticing what sensations there might be in your body in the moment, with the goal of awareness, loosening and letting go of any tension.

- Let your eyes close gently.
- Begin by taking your attention down to your feet.
- Feel your feet, wiggle them a little, then let go.
- Breathe out and feel your breath flow all the way to your feet.
- Breathe in and move your attention up to the calves, knees and thighs.
- Feel what sensations might be there, let them roll out, let them go as you breathe out.

- Now focus on the buttocks, the hips and the pelvis.
- Gently breathe in and tense the buttocks, then release them as you breathe out.
- Wiggle the pelvis backwards and forwards.
- Bring your attention up into the belly. You will probably notice it rising and falling a little with each breath.
- Now move your attention up to the chest. Be aware of the movement as you breathe, the chest moving in rhythm with the belly.
- Take your attention down to your hands and fingers.
- Breathe in and out as you stretch your fingers and thumbs.
- Now focus on your forearms, elbows, upper arms and shoulders.
- Feel your shoulders as you raise and lower them a little.
- Breathe in and out and feel a wave of relaxation flowing down through your arms.
- Feel your head as you nod gently, then turn it gently from side to side, loosening and letting go.

- Bring your attention to your jaw and tongue.
- With your lips lightly touching, let your jaw drop a little, give it a wiggle, then let your tongue soften in your mouth and come to rest sitting gently behind your top teeth.
- Breathe.
- Feel your face. Let it soften, then gently raise your eyebrows up and let go.
- Feel your whole body breathe in and out and let go.
- Do each exercise as long as you need to or repeat the exercise by scanning all body parts for tension.
- When you are ready, take a deep breath or two, perhaps move your feet a little, then feel your hands move a little, and then let your eyes gently open.

Resonance frequency breathing

Also known as coherent breathing, resonance frequency breathing ranges from 5 to 7bpm (breaths per minute) for adults and 6.5 to 9.5bpm for children. This difference is due to the developmental physical difference in the size of the heart and lungs in adults compared to those in children. To find out your exact rate, you will need to consult a therapist who specialises in this work. However, attempting to slow your rate towards the desired 5–7bpm will still be beneficial.

It is worth noting that you must have learnt to breathe effortlessly and well before trying to reduce your breathing rate. It is not just the slowing of the rate that is important, the volume must also be reduced. I often see clients slow their breathing but also take massive, big breaths in which they are over-breathing and expelling too much CO_2—and we know the result of that.

This is an advanced technique that is best practised under the guidance of a health professional who knows what they are doing. However, you could try to see if you can slow your breath after a period of relaxed breathing at night.

For example, do a body scan and then 5–10 minutes of relaxed breathing, then try to slow your breath. Initially breathe in for a count of two and out for a count of three, which equates to 12bpm. Then try breathing in for a count of three and out for a count of four. This equates to a bpm of 8.5. Slowly progress up to breathing in for a count of four and out for a count of six, which is equivalent to 6bpm. This should feel relaxed and not forced. If you can tolerate this rate, work towards it each night before sleep, as it is the fastest way to calm your system and prepare for a healthy night's sleep.

Note: Should symptoms occur, stop and revert to how you normally breathe.

Stimulation breathing exercises

The aim of these exercises is to activate the nervous system. As you feel comfortable, begin to build up the time to about 30 seconds. This is a useful pick-me-up which you can try using instead of having another cup of coffee.

Cleansing the lungs—removal of stale air

1. Sitting or standing, breathe in through your nose.
2. Purse your lips as if to whistle, then blow.
3. To ensure all the air is out, continue blowing out in short, sharp breaths.
4. Finally, blow out in one big, long breath.
5. Inhale sharply back in through the nose until your lungs are full.
6. Gently release the breath again through pursed lips.

Instant, energising breathing stretches

These stretches provide instant energy by increasing the flow of blood to the brain.

1. Stand with your feet shoulder-width apart.
2. Tail tuck (tilt your pelvis under) then inhale.
3. Lift both arms above your head.
4. Interlock your fingers then stretch up.

5. As you breathe out, let your arms come back down to your sides.
6. Repeat three times.
Or try this one:
1. Stand with your feet shoulder-width apart.
2. Tail tuck (tilt your pelvis under) then inhale.
3. Stretch your arms and shoulder blades forwards at shoulder height.
4. Exhale and stretch your arms forward.
5. Breathe in and pull your shoulder blades together behind your back.
Repeat for a couple of breaths.

Muscle strengthening

Inspiratory muscle training (IMT)

Inspiratory muscle training involves breathing against a load to make the inspiratory muscles work harder. This training has a long history. During the First World War, soldiers recovering from lung damage as a result of toxic gas inhalation were given thick wads of cotton wool to breathe into in order to strengthen their chest muscles.

There are many types of IMT devices on the market. One of the best researched and strongest is the Powerbreathe, which was developed by Dr Alison McConnell, an exercise physiologist and keen sportswoman. McConnell's initial research involved healthy older people who were experiencing breathlessness. This soon progressed to involve both sportspeople and those suffering from lung conditions. Dr McConnell found that when athletes warmed up their breathing muscles as part of their general pre-competition warm-up, they performed better and recovered more quickly.

During strenuous exercise, the inspiratory muscles can demand as much as 12 per cent of total oxygen uptake and 15 per cent of cardiac output. The theory is that if the breathing muscles are conditioned they will demand less oxygen, leaving more for the other skeletal muscles.

IMT helps with pattern reinforcement and warm-up prior to competition at low- to mid-levels. At higher levels, the IMT strengthens the respiratory muscles. This is believed to decrease breathlessness and decrease 'blood stealing', which occurs when oxygen-rich blood is diverted away from the limbs to power the respiratory muscles.

Note: If you do purchase a device, talk with your therapist about how best to use it. You should also start on a level with an ideal pattern, which must be established before any load training begins.

Breath-hold breathing

These exercises are commonly prescribed by therapists and are freely discussed on the internet. If achieved comfortably and easily, these slow rates will help heart rate, blood pressure and many other bodily functions. They work on the same physiological principles as resonant breathing.

The breath-hold will also assist in retaining CO_2, so it is helpful if anxiety symptoms are present.

The box breath

This practice was devised by former US Navy SEAL commander Mark Divine.

1.   Breathe in through your nose while counting to four slowly.
2.   Hold your breath inside while counting slowly to four.
3.   Slowly exhale for four seconds.

This results in taking five breaths per minute.

Repeat steps one to three at least three times. Ideally, repeat the three steps for four minutes, or until calm returns.

The 4-7-8 breath

This practice was adapted from yoga breathing by American integrative medicine specialist Dr Andrew Weil.

1.   Empty the lungs of air through your mouth.
2.   Place the tongue behind the top front teeth.
3.   Breathe in quietly through the nose for four seconds.
4.   Hold the breath for a count of seven seconds.
5.   Exhale forcefully through the mouth, pursing the lips and

making a 'whoosh' sound for eight seconds.

Repeat the cycle up to four times and no more. This equals approximately three breaths per minute.

Note: Gradually work towards the slow rate—for example, maybe start with 3-3-3—and if these exercises do not feel comfortable, please do not do them. These are only exercises and should not become normal breathing practice. If you are going to use these techniques to help calm your system, please be gentle with the holds and be mindful of the mantra 'when in doubt, breathe out'.

Paced breathing exercises

For people with COPD, lung disease, chronic fatigue or post-COVID malaise, a simple task, such as making your bed, can feel like hard work. For these people, pacing and prioritising are important.

Listen to your body

When you start to feel tired, it is an indication that it's time to stop, pause and breathe. Listen to your body.

Is the pause enough, or is a longer rest and relax required? Do you need to recharge? Pushing yourself into exhaustion is not beneficial. Use the bank account scenario—spend too much and you will go into overdraft, and this will need to be repaid at some time. In this case, it will be through symptoms such as sore, achy muscles, breathlessness and fatigue.

Pacing and cadence

When climbing stairs, take them three steps at a time in a rhythm co-ordinated with your breath. For example, breathe in and step 1-2-3-pause, rest, breathe out and repeat. If you do this, you won't need a long rest at the top of the stairs and you won't feel so tired. Remember to go at your own pace. You may find two steps breathing in and three steps breathing out works better for you, or perhaps you'll prefer a ratio of five steps in and six steps out. Know that even the fittest person can feel breathless if they race upstairs and hold their breath.

Jeni is an Olympic hockey player. She was complaining of breathlessness when going up stairs and when running into her local café to pick up a coffee each morning. She was fit and had been medically checked and there were no organic reasons for her breathlessness.

Jeni was a big breath-holder and would often hold her breath when moving—for example, going up stairs, or jumping out of the car in the morning to get her coffee. With awareness and application of the 'when in doubt, breathe out' mantra, she soon became symptom-free.

Energy-conserving practices

- Work out how many energy units you have for each day. When they have been used, know that spending more will tip the balance. It is your choice. Do ask for help.
- Break activities up into smaller tasks or energy blocks. Clinically, we talk about spoonsful of energy

units. Set a limit for yourself, such as 10 spoons to use each day.

- Take breathing and rest breaks regularly.
- Alternate activities depending on energy requirements. For example, mow half of the lawn then have a cup of tea. When you're well rested, mow the other half of the lawn.
- If you have a major function to attend, plan to do very little the day preceding and the day following it.
- Ask yourself 'What is the most important thing I should be doing?', then try to focus on that.
- Don't hold your breath during any task.
- Push or slide items as much as possible, rather than lifting them.
- Breathe in when standing up, and breathe out when sitting down. Breathe in when you reach for something, and breathe out when returning your arm to your side. These are all the natural rhythms of the body.
- Bend with your knees rather than from your waist.

- Break up tiring tasks with easy ones and more rests.

Clearance methods

Nasal washing

Salt water is a natural wash for the linings of the nasal cavity. The cavity is accustomed to salt water, as tears, which are salty, drain into the nose along the sinuses. It is well known that people who regularly swim in the sea have excellent nasal health.

Nasal wash recipe

This recipe for a nasal wash is an easy, cheap and effective remedy. The salt in this recipe helps to reduce nasal sogginess, while the bicarbonate of soda acts like Teflon so nothing can stick to it.

This rinse can also be used as a mouth gargle when you have a sore throat or just to cleanse the mouth and throat.

1. Dissolve half a teaspoon of rock or sea salt and half a teaspoon of bicarbonate of soda in half a litre of hot, boiled water.

2. Fill a sterilised nasal spray bottle or bulb syringe with the solution, then discard the rest.

3. Spray each nostril morning and evening for two to three days. Aim the nozzle towards the outside corner of the eye of the same side as the nostril being sprayed. You should spray until you feel it hit the back of your throat. For maximum saturation, tilt the spray bottle until it's almost horizontal.

4. Sniff gently, hoick and spit.

5. Spray as required.

The snuffle method

This method suits those who don't like using gadgets or are fed up with them.

1. With clean and dry hands, pour some of the nasal wash solution into the palm of your hand.

2. Closing one nostril, snuffle the saline into your nose.

3. Move the jaw a couple of times to allow movement of the fluid along the sinuses.

4.　Blow out into a tissue. Do not close off one nostril when blowing out, as this may force water back into your ear.

5.　Repeat on the same nostril.

6.　Switch to the other nostril and repeat twice.

If you have a nasal infection, rinse morning and night until the infection improves.

If the water goes into the upper sinuses, you may experience an uncomfortable stinging sensation. While this might be a little unpleasant, it won't cause any damage, so please don't let it deter you. I cannot emphasise enough the importance of healthy, clear passages.

RESOURCES

Further reading

Bartley, Jim and Clifton-Smith, Tania, *Breathing Matters,* Random House, Auckland, 2006

Bradley, Dinah and Clifton-Smith, Tania, *Breathe, Stretch and Move,* Random House, Auckland, 2002

Bradley, Dinah and Clifton-Smith, Tania, *Dynamic Breathing,* Random House, Auckland, 2008

Chaitow, Leon et al, *Recognizing and Treating Breathing Disorders,* Churchill Livingstone, London, 2013

Useful websites

Find a therapist

BradCliff Breathing Therapists
An international community of skilled health professionals trained specifically in breathing dysfunction, breathing

pattern disorders and hyperventilation across the spectrum of presentations, from the child with asthma, to the elite athlete, to the anxious client.

To find a therapist who is medically trained in this field internationally, visit www.bradcliff.com.

Mirimiri and romiromi practitioner

Traditional Māori bodywork and healing.

Jolie Davis, Manawa Ora mirimiri and workshops www.manawaora.org

National societies of physiotherapy

Search the website of your country's society of physiotherapy to find a cardio-respiratory physiotherapist.

Pelvic health physiotherapist

Google search for a pelvic health physiotherapist in your area, the most experienced will be qualified to complete internal examinations.

Physiotherapists working in the area of mental health

The International Organization of Physical Therapy in Mental Health is an international network of physical therapists working in the field of

psychiatry and mental health. www.iop
tmh.org

Physiotherapy for Breathing Pattern Disorders

Breathing dysfunction, breathing pattern disorders and hyperventilation

Breathing Pattern Disorders: information for patients, NHS University of Southampton—www.uhs.nhs.uk/Medi a/UHS-website-2019/Patientinformation/ Respiratory

Breathing-pattern-disorders-patient-i nformation.pdf

This is a British website that provides advice, lists specialist physios by area, and offers its members access to private resources. www.physiotherap yforbpd.org.uk

Breathing Works clinic—www.breathi ngworks.com

Bronchiectasis Toolbox's breathing dysfunction information page—https://b ronchiectasis.com.au/physiotherapy/tech niques/breathing-dysfunction

Severe Asthma Toolkit's dysfunctional breathing information page—https://too

lkit.severeasthma.org.au/co-morbidities/
pulmonary-upper-airways/dysfunctional-
breathing/

Allergies

Allergy New Zealand is a national charity that offers reliable information, education and support so you can manage your or your child's allergy, and live an active and healthy lifestyle. htt p://www.allergy.org.nz/

American College of Allergies Asthma and Immunology. https://acaai.org/

Anxiety

https://www.anxiety.org.nz/

Anxiety and Depressions Association of America https://adaa .org/

ADAA is an international non-profit organisation dedicated to the prevention, treatment and cure of anxiety, depression, OCD, PTSD, and co-occurring disorders through education, practice and research

Anxiety and panic attacks | Mind https://www.mind.org.uk > about-an xiety

Persistent pain

The Empowered Beyond Pain podcast series— https://bodylogic.phy sio/podcast/trailer/

Pain-Ed— Pain-Ed.com

Pain-Ed's mission is to inform both the public and health care practitioners about the latest pain research, and to dispel common myths about pain and provide hope for change.

pain HEALTH— https://painhealth.c sse.uwa.edu.au

This is a website set up by the Western Australian Department of Health, Curtin University, the University of Western Australia and the Musculoskeletal Health Network. It offers clinically supported information, tips and self-management tools to assist in the management of musculoskeletal pain.

COVID-19

Centers for Disease Control and Prevention— www.cdc.gov/coronavirus /2019-nCoV/index.html—The US government's Centers for Disease

Control and Prevention website contains the latest information on COVID-19.

Long Covid Support— www.longcovid.org

Lung disease

Chronic obstructive pulmonary disease (COPD), asthma and bronchiectasis

Asthma + Respiratory Foundation NZ— http://asthmafoundation.org.nz/

Bronchiectasis Toolbox— https://bronchiectasis.com.au

A multidisciplinary resource for the diagnosis and management of bronchiectasis.

COPD International— www.copd-international.com

Global Initiative for Asthma (GINA)— https://ginasthma.org/

GINA was established in 1993 with the goal of disseminating information about asthma.

Global Initiative for Chronic Obstructive Lung Disease (GOLD)— https://goldcopd.org

GOLD aims to raise awareness of chronic obstructive pulmonary disease

(COPD) and to improve prevention and treatment of this lung disease.

Lung Foundation Australia— https://lungfoundation.com.au

Lung Foundation Australia works to improve lung health and reduce the impact of lung disease for all Australians. This website has excellent information sheets for all lung diseases.

Lung Foundation Australia Pulmonary Rehabilitation Toolkit— https://pulmonaryrehab.com.au/

A resource to help health professionals design and deliver an evidence-based pulmonary rehabilitation programme to benefit people managing lung disease.

Severe Asthma Tool Kit, University of Newcastle, Australia— https://toolkit.severeasthma.org.au/

The Asthma Control Test (ACT)— www.asthmacontroltest.com ACT has been proven to be useful for assessing whether asthma is well managed or not.

Women's Health

continence.org.nz

physio.org.nz/how-physio-helps/pelvic-floor-disorders
http://www.pelvicfloorfirst.org.au/
https://www.healthnavigator.org.nz/
pelvicpain.org.au

Suggested products

To improve nasal patency

Nasal dilators

Intake breathing bands help open the nostrils. They are specifically built to withstand high-intensity exercise and are recommended for sport as well as sleep—www.intakebreathing.com

Breathe Right nasal strips—www.breatheright.com

Sinus rinse bottles

NeilMed sinus rinse bottles—http://shop.neilmed.com/Products/Sinus-Rinse

Sputum clearance devices:

These are advised for long-term use by people with chronic productive coughs and sputum. They can also be used in the short term by adults and children with productive coughs; for example, following a cold, bronchitis or an asthma flare-up. Talk with your physiotherapist about which device suits you. Whichever one you choose, ensure you clean it on a regular basis.

The Shaker Medic for clinics, and the Shaker Deluxe and Shaker for Kids for home use are all clinically proven devices. They are available from Powerbreathe—www.powerbreathe.com

AirPhysio mucus clearing oscillating positive expiratory (OPEP) devices—www.airphysio.com/

Aerobika—this is fast becoming a favourite of cardiorespiratory physiotherapists. www.aerobika.us

Airflow control

Flow-ball devices
These are beneficial for people for whom sustained and controlled breathing is a requirement, such as musicians and singers. It is also ideal to encourage children to do breathing exercises as it can be a lot of fun.

www.powerbreathe.com/product/flow ball/

Inspiratory Muscle Training (IMT)
Powerbreathe devices—www.powerbreathe.com

Pulse oximeters

These devices are used to measure oxygen saturation in the blood stream. There are many of these on the market, so do your homework before buying one.

Helpful apps

All the apps included here are free and are ones that I have used for some time.

BellyBio Interactive Breathing

This app plays a tune for you to breathe in time with. It slows your breathing and calms you down. Great for beginners!

Breathe+ Simple Breath Trainer

This is a simple app that shows a breathing wave for you to follow. It has nice visuals to follow, but lacks an expiratory pause.

Heart Rate+ Coherence

This is a technical app that allows you to aim to improve your heart and breathing connection. I recommend discussing this with your therapist before beginning.

Prana Breath

This is an advanced breath control app that allows you to change the timing of each individual breath.

Smiling Mind and Headspace

Both of these apps focus on mindfulness, the practice of non-judgemental awareness that is sweeping the nation!

GLOSSARY

abdomen: The part of the body containing the digestive organs. It lies below the diaphragm and above the pelvis. Sometimes called the belly.

abdominal breathing: Breathing that results from contracting the diaphragm. This type of breathing is marked by expansion of the abdomen rather than the chest.

accessory breathing muscles: The term 'accessory muscles' refers to those that assist, but do not play a primary role, in breathing

active cycle of breathing technique (ACBT): An airway clearance technique used to clear mucus and phlegm.

acute: Severe symptoms that are sudden in onset and/or of short duration.

adrenal suppression: The adrenal gland decreasing or stopping hormone production.

air hunger: A sensation of a strong urge to breathe or feeling of breathlessness.

airway obstruction: A blockage of the airways causing difficulty in breathing.

airways: The tubes that carry air to and from the lungs.

allergen: A substance that can cause an allergic reaction.

Allergic Bronchopulmonary Aspergillosis (ABPA): A severe allergy to the spores of Aspergillus moulds.

anaemia: A condition in which there is a deficiency of red cells or of haemoglobin in the blood, causing pallor and weariness.

anaerobic threshold (AT): The exertion level between **aerobic** and **anaerobic** training. During anaerobic metabolism, the body burns stored sugars to supply the additional energy needed, and lactic acid is produced faster than it can be metabolised.

antibodies: Cells produced by the body's immune system to protect it from harmful substances.

Asperger syndrome (AS): This is a neurodevelopmental disorder characterised by significant difficulties in social interaction and nonverbal communication.

asthma: Inflammation of the airways, resulting in wheezing, coughing, chest tightness and shortness of breath.

beta agonists: A group of drugs that work by telling the muscles around the airways to relax, thus widening the airways.

bicarbonate buffering: A system that manages the acid and base imbalances produced by both normal and abnormal physiology. It assists in the handling of carbon dioxide, the by-product of cellular respiration.

bronchoconstriction: A tightening of the smooth muscle in the airway, which usually occurs in asthma, emphysema and other lung diseases.

cadence: A rhythmic sequence or flow, a measure of rhythmical motion or activity.

carbon dioxide (CO_2): A waste gas given off by the body when energy is used. It is excreted by the lungs.

cardiovascular endurance: Exercise of long duration but low intensity, for example, walking, cycling and swimming. Also called aerobic exercise.

cathartic experience: An emotional release.

cells: The structural units that make up every living organism.

cerebrospinal fluid (CSF): The fluid that cushions and protects the brain.

choking during sport: When an athlete fails to manage anxiety and cope with the demands at a crucial moment, which can lead to a catastrophic drop in performance.

chronic disease: A disease that is long-lasting.

chronic fatigue syndrome (CFS): This is a complicated disorder characterised by extreme fatigue that lasts for at least four to six months.

chronic obstructive pulmonary disease (COPD): A chronic inflammatory lung disease that causes obstructed airflow from the lungs.

coherent rhythm: The continuous change of the heart rate, which is considered the gold standard of calm and body homeostasis.

diaphragm: A dome-shaped layer of muscle that separates the chest cavity from the abdominal cavity. It is responsible for approximately 60–80 per cent of the work during quiet (resting) breathing.

dopamine: A chemical used by the nervous system to send messages between cells, which plays a role in how humans feel pleasure.

dyspnoea: Difficulty in breathing. The sensation of breathlessness.

eczema: Chronic inflammation of the skin.

email apnoea: Shallow breathing or holding your breath without realising it while working or playing in front of a computer screen.

emphysema: A disease in which the air sacs of the lungs have become enlarged, resulting in breathlessness.

endorphins: Chemicals produced by the body that give a feeling of well-being.

exacerbate: To increase in severity.

exercise-induced laryngeal obstruction (EILO): A breathing problem that affects people during exercise, EILO is defined by an inappropriate narrowing of the upper airway at the level of the vocal cords (glottis) and/or supraglottis (above the vocal cords).

expectoration: Coughing or spitting out of phlegm or mucus from the throat or lungs.

gas exchange: The transfer of oxygen from the air sacs (alveoli) to the blood, and of carbon dioxide from the blood to the air sacs.

gastro-oesophageal reflux disease (GORD): A common condition caused when acid from the stomach leaks up into the oesophagus.

haemoglobin: The protein molecule in red blood cells that carries oxygen.

heart rate variability (HRV): Fluctuations in the time intervals between successive heartbeats, which are termed interbeat intervals.

histamine: An organic nitrogenous compound involved in the inflammatory response.

homeostasis: Body balance, in particular at a cellular level.

hypercapnia: High levels of carbon dioxide in the blood.

hyperinflation: Over-inflation of the lungs caused by breathing in before fully breathing out.

hypertension: High blood pressure.

hypoventilation: Slow breathing resulting in increased levels of carbon dioxide in the blood.

hypoxaemia: Low levels of oxygen in the blood.

hypoxia: Insufficient amounts of oxygen reaching the tissues of the body.

inflammation: A localised reaction to injury or infection where part of the body becomes red, swollen, painful and hot.

influenza: A serious infection caused by influenza viruses, which shouldn't be confused with the less serious common cold.

inhaler: A device used to deliver medication to the lungs.

lactic acid: An acid produced in muscles as a by-product of exercise. The respiratory equation helps to remove this, and a build-up can cause painful, sore muscles.

laryngopharyngeal reflux (LPR): A condition in which acid that is made in the stomach travels up the oesophagus and into the throat.

limbic system: An area in the brain that deals with emotions and memory.

mindfulness: Paying attention to the present moment with purpose and without judgement.

mucociliary clearance: The process in which the little hair-like projections in the airways (cilia) move continuously to assist in cleaning and clearing mucus.

mucus: A protective secretion of the mucus membranes which, in the nose, throat and lungs, serves the function of trapping bacteria.

neuropsychophysiology: The study of the scientific relationship between the physical brain and behaviour.

nitric oxide (NO): A colourless gas released in the nasal airways of humans. During inspiration through the nose, this NO will follow the airstream to the lower airways and the lungs.

nostril or nasal patency: A measure of how open the nose is.

otolaryngologists: Physicians who specialise in the treatment and management of diseases and disorders of the ear, nose, throat and related bodily structures.

overwhelm: When we are completely submerged by thoughts and emotions surrounding a situation or live event.

oxygen: Part of the air we breathe, which is necessary for the body to function.

oxygen saturation: The amount of oxygen carried in the blood.

panic attack: The abrupt onset of intense fear or discomfort that reaches a peak within minutes and includes at least four of the following symptoms: palpitations, pounding heart, accelerated heart rate, sweating, trembling or shaking.

panicogen: A chemical that triggers panic.

pH: A measure of acidity and alkalinity.

pneumonia: Inflammation of the lung caused by infection, resulting in air sacs (alveoli) becoming filled with pus.

pneumothorax: Commonly known as a collapsed lung, this involves air leaking into the space between the lung and the chest wall.

post-exertional malaise (PEM): The worsening of symptoms following even minor physical or mental exertion.

postural bronchial drainage: The drainage of fluids from the lungs by means of changing posture.

prefrontal cortex (PFC): The cerebral cortex covering the front part of the frontal lobe. This brain region has been implicated in planning complex cognitive behaviour, personality expression, decision-making, and moderating social behaviour.

pulmonary: Relating to the lungs.

pulse oximetry: A test used to measure oxygen saturation of the blood using a pulse oximeter.

pursed-lipped breathing: A breathing technique designed to make your breaths more effective by making them slower and more controlled.

rapid eye movement sleep (REM sleep or REMS): A unique phase of sleep in mammals and birds, characterised by random rapid movement of the eyes, accompanied by low muscle tone throughout the body.

recovery breathing: A technique used to help breathing return to a more comfortable level after heavy exercise or when breathing is unsettled.

relative energy deficiency in sport (RED-S): The result of insufficient intake and/or excessive energy expenditure.

resonance frequency breathing: A way of breathing (slow, relaxed, abdominal, diaphragmatic breathing at around 5–7 breaths per minute) that has a regulating effect on brain function, the autonomic nervous system and other key body systems such as the circulatory system.

screen apnoea, email apnoea: This occurs when people hold their breath while sitting in front of a screen, causing a drop in oxygen saturation.

self-regulation: This involves controlling one's behaviour, emotions and thoughts.

sputum: A mixture of saliva and mucus coughed up from the respiratory tract.

stridor: A high-pitched sound caused by a blockage in the throat or voice box (larynx).

thegosis: Tooth-sharpening behaviour.

Triune brain theory: This theory suggests the stages of evolution of the brain. First, functions controlling our primal instincts, followed by the limbic system, which is in charge of our emotions, then the neocortex, which is thought to be responsible for rational or objective thought.

ventilation: Getting air into and out of the lungs.

ventilation perfusion ratio: Getting air into and out of the lungs, and the gas exchange from the alveoli to the blood capillaries.

vocal cord dysfunction (VCD) or paradoxical vocal fold movement (PVFM): Occurs when the vocal cords (voice box) do not open correctly.

wheezing: A whistling or rattling breathing sound.

World Health Organization (WHO): A specialised agency of the United Nations responsible for international public health.

ACKNOWLEDGEMENTS

There are many acknowledgements to be made, but the first must go to all the incredible patients I have been privileged to meet and treat over my clinical working career. Some have remained with me, and their journeys have created life-changing experiences not just for them but also for me. It is these people sharing their stories throughout the therapist–client journey that has enabled me to write this book.

Thank you to the colleagues and mentors who have contributed to and moulded my thinking along the way, and there are many of you.

In the early days, my physiotherapy tutors and teachers, in particular Mark Cranswick, taught me to think outside the square.

The UK medical team, whom I worked with in the late 1980s, introduced me to the concept of breathing dysfunction and hyperventilation syndrome.

The International Society for the Advancement of Respiratory

Psychophysiology (ISARP) meetings that sucked every dollar I earnt into international travel in the 1990s. These helped to lay a foundation of knowledge.

Meeting Dinah Morrison (Bradley) was a tipping point for me. Her ground-breaking book *Hyperventilation Syndrome* helped pave the way for the foundation of all our work. We've had many fun and challenging times at our Breathing Works clinic, and as we developed our programme for health professionals—BradCliff Breathing method, a combination of our surnames. Both the clinic and the programme continue to be trailblazers in this field.

Many thanks to the specialists who support our work and the GPs who refer people who have breathing pattern disorders. In particular, I'd like to thank otolaryngologist Dr Jim Bartley, Dr Sven Hansen, the founder of The Resilience Institute, respiratory consultant Dr Adrian Harrison, and clinical psychologist Chris Gilbert, who all share the science and clinical passion in this field. Thank you to the BradCliff team and graduates—'BradGrads'—all of whom I am sure will continue to grow this academic clinical community for the better of patients afflicted by this silent and often overlooked disorder. Thank you also to Caroline Nicolson for her dedication to the field of bronchiectasis research. Liz Childs Pelvic Physiotherapy, Rosemary Mannering, Mental Health Physiotherapy and Lee Gardener work-related physiotherapy.

Rosalba Courtney, osteopath, a comrade in arms. I admire her drive to continue to bring science to this scope of practice and I stand beside her.

A special mention in particular to Brooke and Scott Peirce, Jess DeMars and Pip Windsor. Thanks also to Janet Rowley, with whom I have worked since 2003 and who kindly passed her expert eye over the first draft of this book.

Thank you to Jolie Davis for her insight into Māori bodywork and breathing.

To the Penguin Random House team, especially Margaret Sinclair and Grace Thomas. And to Jo Dalgety for instant editing feedback.

Thanks to my family and friends, especially my girlfriends who allow me to come up for air occasionally and remind me there is a life beyond the science and practice of breathing. To my brothers and parents, who instilled in me there is no such thing as can't, and who have always encouraged and supported me, even if the task looks impossible.

A huge thank you to my husband, Terry, for putting up with my incredibly messy but, I will add, orderly office, and for my absence over the months when writing, and to my children Jess and Ollie, who I cannot imagine life without. You both enrich my being and, as a mother, I learn something about myself and life on a regular basis because of you. I cannot wait to see what future gems unfold.

About the author

Tania Clifton-Smith is an international medical authority, clinician, educator and trailblazer in the field of breathing dysfunction, breathing disorders and hyperventilation. Over 30 years, her clinic has helped some 40,000 clients manage and resolve breathing dysfunction and disorders, allowing them to breathe well and live better.

get rid of workplace stress

BREATHE
STRETCH
& MOVE

Dinah Bradley & Tania Clifton-Smith

Break the cycle of tension and exhaustion in the workplace and learn how to have greater energy through correct breathing.

Workers today are becoming more sedentary. We are thinking more and using our bodies less—we communicate all day with a computer screen, becoming so absorbed that our shoulders tense, our breathing changes, we hold our breath too much and, by the end of the day, we're exhausted.

The exercises in this book will help you restore energy-efficient breathing and improve your energy levels, productivity and work pace. You will learn to run on natural not nervous energy, and your thought patterns will become calm but alert. You will reduce your stress levels naturally and without drugs.

The book includes a number of crucial exercises specifically for high computer users, and more general exercises for all sedentary workers. Then there are exercises to energise you and to reduce anxiety before presentations, meetings and job interviews.

Improve heart health and relieve headaches, asthma and anxiety by breathing well

breathing matters

a New Zealand guide

Dr Jim Bartley FRACS
with Tania Clifton-Smith Dip Phys

Breathing Matters is a revolutionary book from one of New Zealand's top Ear, Nose & Throat surgeons, Dr Jim Bartley and Tania Clifton-Smith, well regarded breathing expert.

The authors believe that good breathing patterns can dramatically improve the lives of people with major diseases such as heart disease, asthma and depression. Breathing well helps us relax, normalises body biochemistry, reduces muscle pain and allows the re-establishment of normal posture and movement.

This book provides advice on breathing techniques, posture, self-massage and stretches that you can adopt to help you breath better and to relieve pain.

Attention to breathing techniques can improve common conditions such as asthma, heart disease, migraine, tension headaches, jaw joint pain, anxiety and depression.

This books is a must for every health practitioner and anyone who wants to improve their health and better understand their body.

For more information about our titles
go to www.penguin.co.nz